Praise for *Failing Forward*

"Failure is the hallmark of success. Without failure there would be no great successes. John Maxwell reveals the secrets for turning everyday failures into the stepping-stones of achievement. With this book, you'll never fear failure again!"

David W. Anderson
Founder and Chairman,
Famous Dave's of America, Inc.

"All of us have experienced professional or personal failures in our lives. This book will encourage you to look at your failures as stepping-stones rather than stop signs. It will help you face your failures with faith and steer you away from dwelling on the facts that caused your failure."

Anne Beiler
Founder, Auntie Anne's
Hand-Rolled Soft Pretzels

"John Maxwell has once again written an incredible book, *Failing Forward*, to help us understand ourselves. Unfortunately, he paints all too clear a picture of how all too often we view failure in the wrong way. Through this book John encourages us to embrace failure and see the value of it in our lives instead of avoiding it. Through incredible stories and wonderful insight, John helps us to see the importance of failure as we proceed on the journey of life. Thanks for helping me see that no matter how difficult life is, "The key to overcoming . . . doesn't lie in changing your circumstances. It's in changing yourself." With all the struggles I've faced in battling cancer and losing a career as a major-league baseball pitcher, thanks for helping me realize the value of *Failing Forward*."

Dave Dravecky
Author, *Comeback*

"One of the greatest attributes of Dr. John Maxwell's books is that they challenge you to grow as a person and reach your maximum potential. *Failing Forward* will inspire you to overcome whatever obstacles you are facing personally and professionally. After reading this book you will be highly motivated to encourage others and add value to their lives."

Greg Horn
Owner, Payless Food Center,
Cynthiana, Kentucky

"Once again John Maxwell has hit a home run! Everything about this book resonates with me because every defining moment of my life has come as the result of adversity or failure. God has used what I thought were setbacks to push me forward in His plan for my life. John Maxwell is absolutely right: 'Failure is a price we pay for success.'"

David Jeremiah
President, Turning Point

D0042988

"In his warm and friendly style, John Maxwell teaches us that our failures and adversities can and should be used to help us 'fail forward.' This should become your handbook on how to make the most of your mistakes."

Barbara Johnson
Author, *He's Gonna Toot,*
and I'm Gonna Scoot

"*Failing Forward* offers fifteen practical steps to help you become the high achiever you were meant to be. I highly endorse these principles and procedures."

Jack Kinder Jr.
Kinder Brothers International

"John Maxwell is a leader's leader who knows what it takes to succeed. The fact that he's devoted an entire book to the topic of failure is a testimony to how vital 'failing forward' is to both success and leadership."

Peter Lowe
Success Strategist and CEO,
Peter Lowe International

"I highly recommend Dr. John C. Maxwell's new book, *Failing Forward*, to anyone, regardless of their occupation. We all experience some form of failure, and Dr. Maxwell shows us how to deal with failures and turn them into successes. He also gives some real-life experiences of successful people to demonstrate how they handled situations by 'failing forward.' Great reading for anyone."

Dan Reeves
Head Coach, Atlanta Falcons

"I have long been a believer in the value of treasure hunting trials. In *Failing Forward*, John Maxwell offers great insight on how to learn and grow from past failures."

Gary Smalley
Author, *Making Love Last Forever*

"John Maxwell has written another classic on dealing with important life issues. *Failing Forward* is his best book yet, and that is saying a lot!"

Pat Williams
Co-Founder, Orlando Magic

"Really successful people fail many times. John Maxwell's *Failing Forward* makes you realize what a regular part of life failure is. He convinces you that you can overcome it, and in the process teaches you how."

Zig Ziglar
Author, *Over the Top*

FAILING
FORWARD

TURNING MISTAKES *into*
STEPPING STONES *for* SUCCESS

John C. Maxwell

Published by
THOMAS NELSON
Since 1798
www.thomasnelson.com

This book is dedicated to
The INJOY Group,
men and women wholeheartedly
committed to the mission of
helping others learn how
to fail forward.

Published in Nashville, Tennessee, by Thomas Nelson. Thomas Nelson is a registered trademark of Thomas Nelson, Inc.

Thomas Nelson, Inc. titles may be purchased in bulk for educational, business, fundraising, or sales promotional use. For information, please email SpecialMarkets@ThomasNelson.com.

The Scripture quotation noted NKJV is from THE NEW KING JAMES VERSION. © 1979, 1980, 1982, Thomas Nelson, Inc., Publishers.

The Scripture quotation noted NIV is from the HOLY BIBLE: NEW INTERNATIONAL VERSION®. © 1973, 1978, 1984 by International Bible Society. Used by permission of Zondervan Publishing House. All rights reserved.

Library of Congress Cataloging-in-Publication Data

Maxwell, John C., 1947–
    Failing forward : turning mistakes into stepping-stones for success / John C. Maxwell.
        p. cm.
    Includes bibliographical references
    ISBN: 978-0-7852-7430-8 (hc)
    ISBN: 978-0-7852-6815-4 (ie)
    ISBN: 978-0-7852-8857-2 (tp)
    1. Success—Psychological aspects. 2. Self-actualization—Case studies. 3. Success in business—Case studies. 4. Failure (Psychology) I. Title.
    BF637.S8 M3416 2000
    158.1—dc21
                                                                    99-059267
                                                                    CIP

Printed in the United States of America.
13   RRD   24

Acknowledgments

Thank you to the wonderful people who helped me create this book:

> Charlie Wetzel, my writer
> Linda Eggers, my executive assistant
> Brent Cole, my research assistant
> Stephanie Wetzel, my proofreader

CONTENTS

Preface: Becoming a REAL Success   ix

1. What's the Main Difference Between People   1
Who Achieve and People Who Are Average?

Mary Kay Ash put her life savings on the line to start her business; then tragedy threatened to overcome her. Instead, she overcame it and built a world-class business in the process. The secret? She possessed the one quality that separates achievers from average people.

Redefining *Failure* and *Success*

2. Get a New Definition of *Failure* and *Success*   11
What is failure? Truett Cathy knew from experience what it was—and wasn't. That's why the little restaurant he founded south of Atlanta, Georgia, has grown into a billion-dollar enterprise.

3. If You've Failed, Are You a Failure?   23
Achievers possess seven qualities that keep them from becoming failures. Erma Bombeck and Daniel Ruettiger possessed them. Do you?

4. You're Too Old to Cry, but It Hurts Too Much to Laugh   35
The Wright Brothers should not have been the first to achieve flight in an airplane. But the man destined to do it gave up before he achieved his dream. What created the difference between them?

5. Find the Exit Off the Failure Freeway   47
What's worse than being stuck in rush-hour traffic? Being stuck on the failure freeway. If you want to succeed, you can't be like Rosie Ruiz. You must learn to find the exit.

Do You Mind Changing Your Mind?

6. No Matter What Happens to You, Failure Is an Inside Job 61

Floodwaters engulfed his store, causing $1 million worth of damage. Most people would have given up, but not Greg Horn. Find out why.

7. Is the Past Holding Your Life Hostage? 73

What would you do if someone built a public monument to your past failure? Arnold Palmer had that happen to him when he was at the top of his game. See how he handled it.

8. Who Is This Person Making These Mistakes? 87

For thirty-five years, the greatest obstacle to John James Audubon's success was John James Audubon. But when he changed himself, his whole world changed with him.

9. Get Over Yourself—Everyone Else Has 99

What did a top psychiatrist suggest for preventing a nervous breakdown? It's the same thing screenwriter Patrick Sheane Duncan brought to life when he wrote Mr. Holland's Opus.

Embracing Failure As a Friend

10. Grasp the Positive Benefits of Negative Experiences 113

Did you know that you can turn adversity into advantage? That's what an obscure boy did, and in the process he became second in command of the most powerful nation on earth.

11. Take a Risk—There's No Other Way to Fail Forward 123

Most people judge whether to take a risk based on their fear or the probability of their success. But not Millie. She approached it the right way. Learn her secret of approaching risk.

12. Make Failure Your Best Friend 137

Why in the world would Beck Weathers call positive an event that cost him his nose, one arm, and the fingers on his remaining hand? Because he understood how to make failure his best friend.

Increasing Your Odds for Success

13. Avoid the Top Ten Reasons People Fail   153

Where do you start when it comes to increasing your odds for success? With yourself, of course. That's what Dan Reiland did—and it changed his life.

14. The Little Difference Between Failure and   167
    Success Makes a Big Difference

He's a household name. You've seen his picture on television. You probably thought he was an actor, but he wasn't. You know him because he embodied the little difference between failure and success.

15. It's What You Do After You Get Back Up That Counts   179

People say that Lee Kuan Yew's name should be up there with that of Churchill, Roosevelt, or Reagan. What has he done to deserve such praise? He helped an entire country fail forward! Learn how he did it.

16. Now You're Ready to Fail Forward   191

When he read his own story in print, Dave Anderson said it was a wonder he never gave up. He's an ordinary guy who is a millionaire today—because he knows how to fail forward. Here are his story and the steps you need to fail forward and be successful.

Notes   205

About the Author   209

Preface

Becoming a
REAL Success

As I speak around the country, people often ask me why I write books. I've been asked that question so many times that I want to give you the answer before you begin reading the first chapter of *Failing Forward*.

I have dedicated my life to adding value to people. It's the reason I teach conferences, record lessons on cassette, create training videos, and write books. It's the reason I lead my organization, The INJOY Group. I want to see people achieve. I want to see each person I meet become a REAL success.

I believe that to succeed, a person needs only four things. You can remember them by thinking of the word *REAL*.

Relationships: The greatest skill needed for success is the ability to get along with other people. It impacts every aspect of a person's life. Your relationships make you or they break you.

Equipping: One of the most significant lessons I've learned is that those closest to you determine the level of your success. If your dreams are great, you achieve them only with a team.

Attitude: People's attitudes determine how they approach life day to day. Your attitude, more than your aptitude, will determine your altitude.

Leadership: Everything rises and falls on leadership. If you desire to lift the lid on your personal effectiveness, the only way to do it is to increase your leadership skills.

If you pick up any one of my books, you can be sure that it seeks to add value in one of these four areas. I've written this particular book to change your *attitude* about failure. Read it, absorb it, and allow it to help you turn your mistakes into stepping-stones for success. My desire is that *Failing Forward* will add value to your life.

1

What's the Main Difference Between People Who Achieve and People Who Are Average?

We are all failures—at least, all the best of us are.

—J. M. BARRIE

What makes achievers excel? Why do some people skyrocket while others plummet? You know what I'm talking about. You can call it luck, blessing, or the Midas touch—call it whatever you want. But the truth is that some people just seem to achieve incredible things in spite of tremendous difficulties: They finish in the top 5 percent in nationwide sales for their company after losing key accounts. They find ingenious ways to increase profits for their department in the face of budget cuts. They earn a graduate degree while raising two children as a single parent. They discover awesome business opportunities while colleagues don't see any at all. Or they recruit winner after winner into their organization despite what looks like an anemic labor pool. It doesn't matter what kind of work they do. Wherever they are, they just seem to make things happen.

Certainly all people like to think of themselves as above average. But achievers seem to leave "average" in the dust—so far behind them that ordinary seems a distant memory.

1

WHAT'S THE ROOT OF ACHIEVEMENT?

What makes the difference? Why do some people achieve so much? Is it . . .

- Family background? Having a good family growing up is something to be grateful for, but it's not a reliable indicator of achievement. High percentages of successful people come from broken homes.

- Wealth? No, some of the greatest achievers come from households of average to below-average means. Wealth is no indicator of high achievement, and poverty is no guarantee of low achievement.

- Opportunity? You know, opportunity is a peculiar thing. Two people with similar gifts, talents, and resources can look at a situation, and one person will see tremendous opportunity while the other sees nothing. Opportunity is in the eye of the beholder.

- High morals? I wish that were the key, but it's not. I've known people with high integrity who achieve little. And I've known scoundrels who are high producers. Haven't you?

- The absence of hardship? For every achiever who has avoided tragedy, there's a Helen Keller who overcame extreme disabilities or a Viktor Frankl who survived absolute horrors. So that's not it either.

No, none of these things are the key. When it comes right down to it, I know of only one factor that separates those who consistently shine from those who don't: *The difference between average people and achieving people is their perception of and response to failure.* Nothing else has the same kind of impact on people's ability to achieve and to accomplish whatever their minds and hearts desire.

WHAT YOU NEVER LEARNED IN SCHOOL

Soccer player Kyle Rote Jr. remarked, "There is no doubt in my mind that there are many ways to be a winner, but there is really only one way to be

> *There is no doubt in my mind that there are many ways to be a winner, but there is really only one way to be a loser and that is to fail and not look beyond the failure.*
>
> —KYLE ROTE JR.

a loser and that is to fail and not look beyond the failure." How people see failure and deal with it—whether they possess the ability to look beyond it and keep achieving—impacts *every aspect* of their lives. Yet that ability seems difficult to acquire. Most people don't know where to start looking to get it.

Even positive people have a tough time learning how to see failure positively. For example, I'm known to be a very positive person. (My book *The Winning Attitude* has been in print for more than fifteen years.) But I haven't always been good at failing forward. I wasn't properly prepared for it. It's certainly not something they tried to teach me in school. And kids today don't get it there either. In fact, the school environment often reinforces people's worst feelings and expectations about failure.

Take a look at some of my previous attitudes toward failure, and see if your experience was similar:

1. I feared failure. An experience I had in college, along with my response to it, is typical of what many students encounter. On the first day of class when I was a freshman, the professor walked into my history of civilization class and boldly declared, "Half of you in this room will not pass this class."

What was my first response? Fear! Up to that time, I had never failed a class. And I did not want to start failing all of a sudden. So the first question I asked myself was, *What does the professor want?* School became a game that I wanted to win.

I recall that I once memorized eighty-three dates for a test in that class because my teacher believed that if you could cite the dates, you had mastered the material. I got an A on the test, but three days later, I had forgotten all of the information. I managed to avoid the failure I had feared, but I had not really accomplished anything.

2. I misunderstood failure. What is failure? As a child, I thought it was a

3

percentage. Sixty-nine and lower meant failure. Seventy and above signified success. That thinking didn't help me. Failure isn't a percentage or a test. It's not a single event. It's a process.

3. I was unprepared for failure. When I graduated from college with my bachelor's degree, I finished in the top 5 percent of my class. It didn't mean a thing. I had played the school game successfully, and I had absorbed a lot of information. But I wasn't at all prepared for what was ahead of me.

I found that out in my first job. As the pastor in a small rural church, I worked very hard that first year. I did everything the people might expect of me and then some. But to be honest, I was as concerned about getting everyone to like me as I was with helping people.

In the type of church I led, each year the people voted to decide whether to allow the leader to keep his job. And many of the leaders I knew over the years loved to brag about the unanimous affirming votes they received from their people. My expectations were high as I prepared to receive my first unanimous vote. Imagine my surprise when the votes came back 31 yeses, 1 no, and 1 abstention. I was devastated.

After I went home that night, I called my father, who was a veteran pastor, former district superintendent in the denomination, and college president.

"Dad," I lamented, "I can't believe it. I worked so hard for those people. I've done everything I can." I was at the point of tears. "Somebody actually voted against me and wanted me to leave the church! And an abstention is as good as a no. Should I leave and go to another church?"

To my shock, I heard laughter on the other end of the phone.

"No, son, stay there," my dad said as he chuckled. "That's probably the best vote you'll ever receive."

A New Course

At that moment I realized what an unrealistic view I had of success and failure. If anything, my college experience had reinforced the wrong notions I had about failure. And as I've helped leaders to grow and develop through the years, I've seen that most people are in the same boat.

In *Leadership Magazine,* J. Wallace Hamilton states, "The increase of sui-

> *People are training for*
> *success when they should*
> *be training for failure.*
> *Failure is far more*
> *common than success;*
> *poverty is more prevalent*
> *than wealth; and*
> *disappointment more*
> *normal than arrival.*
>
> —J. WALLACE HAMILTON

cides, alcoholics, and even some forms of nervous breakdowns is evidence that many people are training for success when they should be training for failure. Failure is far more common than success; poverty is more prevalent than wealth; and disappointment more normal than arrival."

Training for failure! That is a great concept, and it's the idea that prompted me to write this book. Right now you are getting the chance to sign up with me for a class you were never offered in school. I want to help you train for failure. I want you to learn how to confidently look the prospect of failure in the eye and move forward anyway. Because in life, the question is not *if* you will have problems, but *how* you are going to deal with your problems. Are you going to fail forward or backward?

PUTTING A NEW FACE ON OBSTACLES

When I think of people who were able to look trouble in the eye and forge ahead, one of the first who comes to mind is Mary Kay Ash. She has built quite an organization. During the last four or five years, I've had many opportunities to speak to the people in her cosmetics company about leadership. In fact, as I travel around the country doing conferences and seminars, it seems that no matter where I speak, there are always at least a dozen Mary Kay consultants in attendance.

I admire Mary Kay. She overcame a lot of obstacles in her career, and she never let failure get the better of her. Mary Kay's first career was in direct sales, and she was quite successful. But she also found that it was difficult for a woman to progress in the corporate world, especially in the 1950s and early 1960s—even after twenty-five years of success. She says,

5

I had worked my way up to being a member of the board of the company I was with only to find that, even though our sales force was made up entirely of women, governed by an all male board, my opinions were of no value. I constantly heard, "Mary Kay, you are thinking like a woman again!" I felt rejection in the worst form. So I decided to retire.[1]

Her retirement didn't last long. By the time a month passed, she was stir-crazy. She was ready to start her own business. If she was going to encounter obstacles, they would be there only because she brought them on herself. She decided on a cosmetics business that would give every woman who worked in it unlimited opportunities. She purchased the formulas to the best beauty products she'd ever found, worked up a marketing plan, and prepared to set up a corporation.

TROUBLE!

It didn't take long for her to hit her first obstacle. When she visited her attorney to make legal arrangements for the corporation, he insulted her and predicted her failure. "Mary Kay," he said, "if you are going to throw away your life savings, why don't you just go directly to the trash can? It will be so much easier than what you are proposing." Her accountant spoke to her in similar terms.

Despite their attempts to discourage her, she moved ahead. She sank her $5,000 life savings into her new business—every cent she had. She put her husband in charge of the administrative side of things as she worked feverishly to prepare the products, design the packaging, write the training materials, and recruit consultants. They were making wonderful progress. But then a month before she was to open for business, her husband died of a heart attack right at their kitchen table.

Most people would never have been able to go on after that. They would have accepted defeat and faded away. But not Mary Kay. She kept going, and on September 13, 1963, she launched her business. Today, the company has more than $1 billion in annual sales, employs 3,500 people, and empowers 500,000 direct-sales consultants in 29 markets worldwide.[2] And

Mary Kay Ash has received just about every award an entrepreneur could dream of. Despite adverse circumstances, obstacles, and hardships, she failed forward.

THE IMPOSSIBLE QUESTION

When I was growing up, one of the questions I used to hear from motivational speakers was this: "If the possibility of failure were erased, what would you attempt to achieve?"

> *If your perception of and response to failure were changed, what would you attempt to achieve?*

That seemed to me to be an intriguing question. At the time it prompted me to look ahead to life's possibilities. But then one day I realized that it was really a bad question. Why? Because it takes a person's thinking down the wrong track. There is no achievement without failure. To even imply that it might be possible gives people the wrong impression. So here's a better question: If your perception of and response to failure were changed, what would you attempt to achieve?

I don't know what obstacles you are facing in your life right now. But whatever they are doesn't matter. What *does* matter is that your life can change if you're willing to look at failure differently. You have the potential to overcome any problems, mistakes, or misfortunes. All you have to do is learn to fail forward. If you are ready to do that, turn the page and let's go!

Your First Step to Failing Forward:

Realize There Is One Major Difference Between Average People and Achieving People

Look at the way any achiever approaches negative experiences, and you can learn a lot about how to fail forward. Read through these two lists, and determine which one describes your approach to failure:

Failing Backward	Failing Forward
• Blaming Others	• Taking Responsibility
• Repeating the Same Mistakes	• Learning from Each Mistake
• Expecting Never to Fail Again	• Knowing Failure Is a Part of Progress
• Expecting to Continually Fail	• Maintaining a Positive Attitude
• Accepting Tradition Blindly	• Challenging Outdated Assumptions
• Being Limited by Past Mistakes	• Taking New Risks
• Thinking *I am a Failure*	• Believing Something Didn't Work
• Quitting	• Persevering

Think about a recent setback you experienced. How did you respond? No matter how difficult your problems were, the key to overcoming them doesn't lie in changing your circumstances. It's in changing yourself. That in itself is a process, and it begins with a desire to be teachable. If you're willing to do that, then you'll be able to handle failure. From this moment on, make a commitment to do whatever it takes to fail forward.

Step to Failing Forward:

1. Realize there is one major difference between average people and achieving people.

Redefining *Failure* and *Success*

2

Get a New Definition of *Failure* and *Success*

*The difference between greatness and mediocrity is
often how an individual views a mistake.*

—NELSON BOSWELL

On August 6, 1999, a major-league baseball player stepped up to home plate in Montreal and made another out—the 5,113th of his professional career. That's a lot of trips to the batter's box without a hit! If a player made all of those outs consecutively, and he averaged four at bats per game, he would play eight seasons (1,278 games straight) without ever reaching first base!

Was the player discouraged that night? No. Did he think he had failed himself or his team? No. You see, earlier in the same game, in his first plate appearance, that player had reached a milestone that only twenty-one other people in the history of baseball have ever achieved. He had made his 3,000th hit. That player was Tony Gwynn of the San Diego Padres.

During that game, Tony got on base with hits four times in five tries. But that's not the norm for him. Usually he *fails* to get a hit two times out of every three attempts. Those results may not sound very encouraging, but if you know baseball, you recognize that Tony's ability to succeed consistently only one time in three tries has made him the greatest hitter of his generation. And Tony recognizes that to get his hits, he has to make a lot of outs.

I've been a Tony Gwynn fan for more than a decade. When I lived in San Diego, I had season tickets to the Padres' games. I saw him play in his first game there. And I've continued to follow his career closely. As he approached hit number 3,000, I knew I wanted to be at the game when he achieved that feat.

On the day he was expected to achieve that milestone, I had just finished teaching leadership at a conference in Chicago, and I was to be speaking in Philadelphia the next day. I scrambled to change my plane tickets. Then I called my son-in-law, Steve, who was going to be at the next conference with me, to invite him along. And each of us hopped on a plane to Montreal for the game.

As I traveled, I knew our schedule would be tight, but I figured we could make it. When we arrived at the airport, everything looked great. But after getting off the plane, Steve got tied up in customs. With the clock ticking away, I was pretty sure that we were going to miss Tony's first at bat. And sure enough, by the time we reached the stadium, he had already batted and hit number 3,000.

HOW DO YOU DEFINE *FAILURE*?

When we realized that we were probably going to miss Tony's historic moment, did we give up? No. When we got to the stadium and *knew* we had missed it, did we turn around and go home? No. Did I think I had failed when I tried to buy a program but learned that the vendors had already sold out of them? No. You see, we were just glad to be a part of the celebration. And like Tony, who keeps

> *One of the greatest problems people have with failure is that they are too quick to judge isolated situations in their lives and label them as failures. Instead, they need to keep the bigger picture in mind.*

hanging in there until he gets his hits, we were rewarded. Late in the game when Tony hit a foul ball into the stands, I got it. A few weeks later Tony signed the ball for me, and now I have a souvenir from his 3,000-hit game.

One of the greatest problems people have with failure is that they are too quick to judge isolated situations in their lives and label them as failures. Instead, they need to keep the bigger picture in mind. Someone like Tony Gwynn doesn't look at an out that he makes and think of failure. He sees it within the context of the bigger picture. His perspective leads to perseverance. His perseverance brings longevity. And his longevity gives him opportunities for success.

FAILURE IS NOT . . .

Changing your perspective on failure will help you to persevere—and ultimately achieve your desires. So how should you judge failure? Let's start by taking a look at seven things failure is *not:*

1. People Think Failure Is Avoidable—It's Not

Everybody fails, errs, and makes mistakes. You've heard the saying "To err is human, to forgive divine." Alexander Pope wrote that more than 250 years ago. And he was only paraphrasing a saying that was common 2,000 years ago, during the time of the Romans. Things today are the same as they were then: If you're a human being, you're going to make mistakes.

You're probably familiar with Murphy's Law and the Peter Principle. Recently I came across something called Rules for Being Human. I think the list describes well the state we're in as people:

Rule #1: You will learn lessons.

Rule #2: There are no mistakes—only lessons.

Rule #3: A lesson is repeated until it is learned.

Rule #4: If you don't learn the easy lessons, they get *harder.*
        (Pain is one way the universe gets your attention.)

Rule #5: You'll know you've learned a lesson when your actions change.

You see, writer Norman Cousins was right when he said, "The essence of man is imperfection." Know that you're going to make mistakes.

2. People Think Failure Is an Event—It's Not

Growing up, I thought that failure came in a moment. The best example I can think of is taking a test. If you got an F, it meant you failed. But I've come to realize that failure is a process. If you flunk a test, it doesn't mean you failed a one-time event. The F shows that you neglected the process leading up to the test.

In 1997, I wrote a book called *The Success Journey*. It offers an overview on what it means to be successful. In it I define *success* in these terms:

> Knowing your purpose in life
> Growing to reach your potential
> Sowing seeds that benefit others

The thesis of the book is that success is not a destination—not a place where you arrive one day. Instead, it is the journey you take. And whether you succeed comes from what you do day to day. In other words, success is a process.

Failure works the same way. It's not someplace you arrive. Just as success is not an event, neither is failure. It's how you deal with life along the way. No one can conclude that he has failed until he breathes his last breath. Until then, he's still in process, and the jury is still out.

3. People Think Failure Is Objective—It's Not

When you err—whether you miscalculate crucial figures, miss a deadline, blow a deal, make a poor choice concerning your children, or otherwise fumble a ball—what determines whether that action was a failure? Do you look at the size of the problem it causes or the amount of money it costs you or your organization? Is it determined by how much heat you have to take from your boss or by the criticism of your peers? No. Failure isn't determined that way. The answer is that *you* are the only person who

> **You are the only person who can really label what you do a failure.**

can really label what you do a failure. It's subjective. Your perception of and response to your mistakes determine whether your actions are failures.

Did you know that entrepreneurs almost never get their first business off the ground? Or their second? Or their third? According to Tulane University business professor Lisa Amos, the average for entrepreneurs is 3.8 failures before they finally make it in business. They are not deterred by problems, mistakes, or errors. Why? Because they don't see setbacks as failures. They recognize that three steps forward and two steps back *still* equals one step forward. And as a result, they overcome the average and become achievers.

4. People Think Failure Is the Enemy—It's Not

Most people try to avoid failure like the plague. They're afraid of it. But it takes adversity to create success. NBA coach Rick Pitino states it even more strongly. "Failure is good," he says. "It's fertilizer. Everything I've learned about coaching I've learned from making mistakes."

People who see failure as the enemy are captive to those who conquer it. Herbert V. Brocknow believes, "The fellow who never makes a mistake takes his orders from one who does." Observe any high achiever, and you'll discover a person who doesn't see a mistake as the enemy. That's true in any endeavor. Musicologist Eloise Ristad emphasizes that "when we give ourselves permission to fail, we at the same time give ourselves permission to excel."

5. People Think Failure Is Irreversible—It's Not

There's an old saying in Texas: "It doesn't matter how much milk you spill as long as you don't lose your cow." In other words, mistakes are not irreversible. Keep everything in perspective. The problems come when you see only the spilled milk and not the bigger picture. People who correctly see failure take it in stride.

Mistakes don't make them want to give up.

Success doesn't make them think that they are set up.

Every event—whether good or bad—is one small step in the process of living. Or as Tom Peters acknowledges, "If silly things were not done, intelligent things would never happen."

6. People Think Failure Is a Stigma—It's Not

Mistakes are not permanent markers. I love the perspective of the late Senator Sam Ervin Jr., who remarked, "Defeat may serve as well as victory to shake the soul and let the glory out." That's the way we need to look at failure.

When you make mistakes, don't let them get you down. And don't let yourself think of them as stigmas. Make each failure a step to success.

> *The average for entrepreneurs is 3.8 failures before they finally make it in business.*

7. People Think Failure Is Final—It's Not

Even what may appear to be a huge failure doesn't need to keep you from achieving. Consider the story of Sergio Zyman. He was the mastermind behind New Coke, something that marketing consultant Robert McMath sees as one of the greatest product failures of all time.[1] Zyman, who successfully introduced Diet Coke, believed that Coca-Cola needed to

Steps to Success

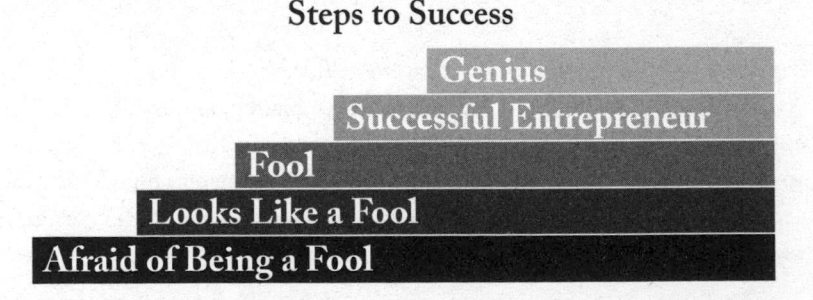

Genius

Successful Entrepreneur

Fool

Looks Like a Fool

Afraid of Being a Fool

act boldly to reverse its twenty-year market decline against its rival, Pepsi. His solution was to stop offering the drink that had been popular for nearly one hundred years, change the formula, and offer it as New Coke. The move was an abysmal failure that lasted seventy-nine days in 1985 and cost the company about $100 million. People hated New Coke. And it caused Zyman to leave the company.

But Zyman's problems with New Coke didn't keep him down. Years later when asked if the venture was a mistake, Zyman answers, "No, categorically."

A failure? "No."

A blunder, a misstep, a bust? "Another word between 'bust' and, uh, something else," he replies. "Now if you say to me, 'The strategy that you guys embarked on didn't work,' I'll say, 'Yeah, absolutely it didn't work.' But the totality of the action ended up being positive." Ultimately the return of Coca-Cola Classic made the company stronger.

Zyman's assessment was confirmed by Roberto Goizueta, the late chairman and chief executive of the Coca-Cola Company. He rehired Zyman at Coca-Cola in 1993. "Judge the results," said Goizueta. "We get paid to produce results. We don't get paid to be right."[2]

IT'S ALL IN HOW YOU LOOK AT IT

If you tend to focus on the extremes of success and failure and to fixate on particular events in your life, try to put things into perspective. When you do, you'll be able to share the philosophy of someone such as the apostle Paul, who was able to say, "I have learned in whatever state I am, to be content."[3] And that was saying a lot, considering that Paul had been shipwrecked, whipped, beaten, stoned, and imprisoned. Throughout everything, his faith enabled him to maintain perspective. He realized that as long as he was doing what he was supposed to do, his being labeled success or failure by others really didn't matter.

Every person's life is filled with errors and negative experiences. But know this:

Errors become mistakes
when we perceive them and respond to them incorrectly.

Mistakes become failures
when we *continually* respond to them incorrectly.

People who fail forward are able to see errors or negative experiences as a regular part of life, learn from them, and then move on. They persevere in order to achieve their purpose in life.

Washington Irving once commented, "Great minds have purposes; others have wishes. Little minds are subdued by misfortunes; but great minds rise above them."

The terrible truth is that all roads to achievement lead through the land of failure. It has stood firmly between every human being who had a dream and the realization of that dream. The good news is that anyone can make it through failure. That's why author Rob Parsons maintained that "tomorrow belongs to the failures."

Too many people believe that the process is supposed to be easy. The prolific American inventor Thomas Edison observed that attitude among people. And this is how he responded to it:

> *Errors become mistakes when we perceive them and respond to them incorrectly. Mistakes become failures when we **continually** respond to them incorrectly.*

Failure is really a matter of conceit. People don't work hard because, in their conceit, they imagine they'll succeed without ever making an effort. Most people believe that they'll wake up some day and find themselves rich. Actually, they've got it half right, because eventually they do wake up.

Each of us has to make a choice. Are we going to sleep life away, avoiding failure at all costs? Or are we going to wake up and realize this: *Failure is simply a price we pay to achieve success.* If we learn to embrace that new definition of failure, then we are free to start moving ahead—and failing forward.

MOVING FORWARD ON THE HEELS OF TRAGEDY

Over dinner, I heard a great story about the price someone paid to achieve success. It all started when I arranged for two friends to meet. Last year when speaking for Auntie Anne's Pretzels, I was talking to Anne Beiler, the company's founder. As we talked, she mentioned in passing that one of her heroes is Truett Cathy, the founder of the Chick-fil-A restaurant chain.

"Would you like to meet him?" I asked.

"You know him?" Anne responded, a little surprised.

"I sure do," I answered. When we moved my company, The INJOY Group, to Atlanta in 1997, Truett and his son Dan Cathy took all of us under their wings. "They're wonderful friends. I'll arrange for all of us to have dinner together."

I immediately set a date, and soon afterward my wife, Margaret, and I had Truett Cathy, Anne and Jonas Beiler, and Dan and Rhonda Cathy over to dinner. We had a wonderful time. I was amazed as Anne and Dan (who is the president of Chick-fil-A International) openly exchanged trade information about their businesses.

I was pleased because I could tell they were enjoying a good connection. But the highlight of the evening for me was hearing Truett Cathy tell the story of his start in the restaurant business and how that led to the founding of Chick-fil-A.

HOW IT ALL BEGAN

Truett's description of his childhood activities showed me that he was a born entrepreneur. As a second grader, he discovered that he could buy a six-pack of Cokes for a quarter, sell them for a nickel apiece, and make a 20 percent profit. It wasn't long before he was buying soft drinks by the case, icing them down, and increasing his revenue and profit. When the weather turned cold and drink sales lagged, he sold magazines. Then at age eleven, he started helping a neighbor with his paper route. By age twelve, he had his own route.

Like many young men of his era, Truett went into the army. When he was discharged in 1945, he was ready to pursue opportunity. What appealed to him was a restaurant, and his dream was to work with Ben, one of his brothers. After learning a little about the business, they scraped together some money, located a site, built a restaurant, and opened it as the Dwarf Grill (later the Dwarf House) in Hapeville, Georgia, on the south side of Atlanta. It was open twenty-four hours, six days a week, and though it required an incredible amount of work, it was profitable from the first week. But it wouldn't be long before Truett faced the first of several major setbacks.

TRAGIC LOSSES

The first came early, only three years after opening the restaurant. Truett's two brothers were in a small private plane that crashed on the way to Chattanooga, Tennessee. Both of them died. Losing a business partner is tough. Losing both brothers was horrible. Truett was devastated. Once he got over the emotional shock, he went on alone. A year later, he paid Eunice, his brother Ben's widow, for her share in the business. A year after that, he opened a second restaurant.

By then things were going pretty well. Then one night he was awakened by a phone call; there was a fire at his second restaurant location. He dashed off to see what could be done, but when he arrived, he discovered that the fire had totally destroyed the operation. That alone was bad enough. Worse was the fact that he had practically no insurance.

Within but a few weeks Truett faced another debilitating setback. He discovered that he had polyps in his colon that would have to be removed. The timing couldn't be worse. Instead of rebuilding his restaurant, he went in for surgery. One operation turned into two, and much to his dismay, he was out of action for several months—an eternity for an energetic businessman like him.

TURNING LEMONS INTO LEMONADE . . . AND CHICKEN SANDWICHES

What does an active entrepreneur do when he's stuck in bed for months at a time? If he's Truett Cathy, he comes up with a million-dollar idea. The time Truett spent out of commission inspired him to play with a new concept. He had always loved chicken, and it had been an important part of the Dwarf House's fare. For a while the restaurant had offered a boneless chicken breast on its menu. *What would happen,* he wondered, *if I took that chicken breast, seasoned and fried it just right, and put it on a bun with the right condiments?* The answer became the Chick-fil-A Sandwich and the start of one of the largest privately owned restaurant chains in the world.

Today Truett Cathy is credited with inventing the chicken sandwich in the fast-food industry. Chick-fil-A operates more than nine hundred restaurants across the country and has a 200,000-square-foot headquarters that sits on seventy-three acres just south of Atlanta. In the year 2000, it became a billion-dollar company. It is one of the most successful operations in the restaurant business, selling millions of chicken sandwiches and countless gallons of its famous fresh-squeezed lemonade. The business continues growing. Yet it never would have come to pass if Truett Cathy had not experienced the setbacks he did, maintained his perspective, and realized that a few negative experiences don't make for failure.

> *Many of life's failures are people who did not realize how close they were to success when they gave up.*
>
> —THOMAS EDISON

Thomas Edison believed, "Many of life's failures are people who did not realize how close they were to success when they gave up." If you can change the way you see failure, you gain the strength to keep running the race. Get a new definition of *failure*. Regard it as the price you pay for progress. If you can do that, you will put yourself in a much better position to fail forward.

Your Second Step to Failing Forward:
Learn a New Definition of *Failure*

How can you help yourself learn a new definition of *failure* and develop a different perspective concerning failure and success? By making mistakes. Chuck Braun of Idea Connection Systems encourages trainees to think differently through the use of a mistake quota. He gives each student a quota of thirty mistakes to make for each training session. And if a student uses up all thirty? He receives another thirty. As a result, the students relax, think of mistakes in a whole new light, and begin learning.

As you approach your next big project or assignment, give yourself a reasonable mistake quotient. How many mistakes should you expect to achieve? Twenty? Fifty? Ninety? Give yourself a quota, and try to hit it before bringing the task to completion. Remember, mistakes don't define *failure*. They are merely the price of achievement on the success journey.

Steps to Failing Forward:

1. Realize there is one major difference between average people and achieving people.

2. Learn a new definition of *failure*.

3

If You've Failed, Are You a Failure?

Failure isn't so bad if it doesn't attack the heart.
Success is all right if it doesn't go to the head.
—GRANTLAND RICE

In an interview years ago, David Brinkley asked advice columnist Ann Landers what question she most frequently receives from readers. Her answer: "What's wrong with me?"

Landers's response reveals a lot about human nature. Many people wrestle with feelings of failure, the most damaging being doubtful thoughts about themselves. At the heart of those doubts and feelings is one central question: Am I a failure? And that's a problem because I believe it's nearly impossible for any person to believe he is a failure and fail forward at the same time.

It seems that advice columnists (such as Ann Landers) and humor writers recognize that keeping a good perspective of yourself is important to overcoming adversity and mistakes. The late Erma Bombeck, who wrote a widely syndicated weekly humor column until a few weeks before her death in 1996, had a firm grasp on what it meant to persevere and fail forward without taking failure too personally.

FROM NEWSPAPER COPY GIRL TO
TIME MAGAZINE COVER GIRL

Erma Bombeck traveled a road that was filled with adversity, starting with her career. She was drawn to journalism early in life. Her first job was as a copy girl at the Dayton *Journal-Herald* when she was a teenager. But when she went off to college at Ohio University, a guidance counselor advised her, "Forget about writing." She refused. Later she transferred to the University of Dayton and in 1949 graduated with a degree in English. Soon afterward she began working as a writer—for the obituary column and the women's page.

That year adversity carried over into her personal life. When she got married, one of her deepest desires was to become a mother. But much to her dismay, her doctors told her she was incapable of having children. Did she give up and consider herself a failure? No, she and her husband explored the possibility of adoption, and then they adopted a daughter.

Two years later, a surprised Erma became pregnant. But even that brought her more difficulties. In four years, she experienced four pregnancies, but only two of the babies survived.

In 1964, Erma was able to convince the editor of a small neighborhood newspaper, the *Kettering-Oakwood Times,* to let her write a weekly humor column. Despite the pitiful $3 per article she was paid, she kept writing. And that opened a door for her. The next year she was offered the opportunity to write a three-times-a-week column for her old employer, the Dayton *Journal-Herald.* By 1967, her column was syndicated and carried by more than nine hundred newspapers.

For slightly more than thirty years Erma wrote her humor column. During that time, she published fifteen books, was recognized as one of the twenty-five most influential women in America, appeared frequently on the television show *Good Morning America,* was featured on the cover of *Time* magazine, received innumerable honors (such as the American Cancer Society's Medal of Honor), and was awarded fifteen honorary degrees.

MORE THAN HER SHARE OF PROBLEMS

But during that span of time, Erma Bombeck also experienced incredible troubles and trials including breast cancer, a mastectomy, and kidney failure. And she wasn't shy about sharing her perspective on her life experiences:

> I speak at college commencements, and I tell everyone I'm up there and they're down there, not because of my successes, but my failures. Then I proceed to spin all of them off—a comedy record album that sold two copies in Beirut . . . a sitcom that lasted about as long as a donut in our house . . . a Broadway play that never saw Broadway . . . book signings where I attracted two people: one who wanted directions to the restroom and the other who wanted to buy the desk.
>
> What you have to tell yourself is, "I'm not a failure. I failed at doing something." There's a big difference. . . . Personally and career-wise, it's been a corduroy road. I've buried babies, lost parents, had cancer, and worried over kids. The trick is to put it all in perspective . . . and that's what I do for a living.[1]

That point of view kept Erma Bombeck down to earth. (She liked to refer to herself as "a former homeroom mother and obituary writer.") It also kept her going—and writing—through the disappointments, the pain, the surgeries, and the daily kidney dialysis until her death at age sixty-nine.

> *Tell yourself, "I'm not a failure. I failed at doing something." There's a big difference.*

EVERY GENIUS COULD HAVE BEEN A "FAILURE"

Every successful person is someone who failed, yet never regarded himself as a failure. For example, Wolfgang Mozart, one of the geniuses of musical composition, was told by Emperor Ferdinand that his opera *The Marriage of Figaro* was "far too noisy" and contained "far too many notes." Artist Vincent van Gogh, whose paintings now set records for the sums they bring at auction, sold only one painting in his lifetime. Thomas Edison, the most prolific inventor in history, was considered unteachable as a youngster. And Albert Einstein, the greatest thinker of our time, was told by a Munich schoolmaster that he would "never amount to much."

I think it's safe to say that all great achievers are given multiple reasons to believe they are failures. But in spite of that, they persevere. In the face of adversity, rejection, and failings, they continue believing in themselves and refuse to consider themselves failures.

> *All great achievers are given multiple reasons to believe they are failures. But in spite of that, they persevere.*

FAILING FORWARD IS NOT FALSE SELF-ESTEEM

In the last twenty years, as educators in the United States have watched students' test scores plummet and their desire to learn decline, they have tried to find ways to reverse those trends. One popular theory states that the best way to improve children's ability is to puff up their self-esteem. When educators observed that high achievers possessed confidence, they theorized that if they simply built self-esteem, competence would follow. But that approach has backfired on them. Researchers have found that simply building children's egos breeds many negative traits: indifference to excellence, inability to overcome adversity, and aggressiveness toward people who criticize them.[2]

Now, I place high value on praising people, especially children. In fact, I believe that people live up to your level of expectations. But I also believe that you have to base your praise on truth. You don't make up nice things to say about others. Here's the approach I use to encourage and lead others:

Value people.
Praise effort.
Reward performance.

I use that method with everyone. I even use a form of it with myself. When I'm working, I don't give myself a reward until after the job is finished. When I approach a task or project, I give it my very best, and no matter what the results are, I have a clear conscience. I have no problem sleeping at night. And no matter where I fail or how many mistakes I make, I don't let it devalue my worth as a person. As the saying goes, "God uses people who fail—'cause there aren't any other kind around."

Like many people, you may have a hard time maintaining a positive mind-set and preventing yourself from feeling like a failure. But know this: It is possible to cultivate a positive attitude about yourself, no matter what circumstances you find yourself in or what kind of history you have.

SEVEN ABILITIES NEEDED TO FAIL FORWARD

Here are seven abilities of achievers that enable them to fail, not take it personally, and keep moving forward:

1. Achievers Reject Rejection

Author James Allen states, "A man is literally what he thinks, his character being the complete sum of all his thought." That's why it's important to make sure your thinking is on the right track.

People who don't give up keep trying because they don't base their self-worth on their performance. Instead, they have an internally based self-image. Rather than say, "I am a failure," they say, "I missed that one," or "I made a mistake."

Psychologist Martin E. Seligman believes we have two choices when we fail: We can internalize or externalize our failure. "People who blame themselves when they fail . . . think they are worthless, talentless, unlovable," says Seligman. "People who blame external events do not lose self-esteem when bad events strike."[3] To keep the right perspective, take responsibility for your actions, but don't take failure personally.

2. Achievers See Failure As Temporary

People who personalize failure see a problem as a hole they're permanently stuck in. But achievers see any predicament as temporary. For example, take the case of United States President Harry S. Truman. In 1922, he was thirty-eight years old, in debt, and out of work. In 1945, he was the most powerful leader of the free world, occupying the highest office in the land. If he had seen failure as permanent, he would have remained stuck and never would have kept trying and believing in his potential.

> *When achievers fail, they see it as a momentary event, not a lifelong epidemic.*

3. Achievers See Failures As Isolated Incidents

Author Leo Buscaglia once talked about his admiration for cooking expert Julia Child: "I just love her attitude. She says, 'Tonight we're going to make a soufflé!' And she beats this and whisks that, and she drops things on the floor . . . and does all these wonderful human things. Then she takes the soufflé and throws it in the oven and talks to you for a while. Finally, she says, 'Now it's ready!' But when she opens the oven, the soufflé just falls flat as a pancake. But does she panic or burst into tears? No! She smiles and says, 'Well, you can't win them all. Bon appetit!'"

When achievers fail, they see it as a momentary event, not a lifelong epidemic. It's not personal. If you want to succeed, don't let any single incident color your view of yourself.

4. Achievers Keep Expectations Realistic

The greater the feat you desire to achieve, the greater the mental preparation required for overcoming obstacles and persevering over the long haul. If you want to take a stroll in your neighborhood, you can reasonably expect to have few, if any, problems. But that's not the case if you intend to climb Mount Everest.

It takes time, effort, and the ability to overcome setbacks. You have to approach each day with reasonable expectations and not get your feelings hurt when everything doesn't turn out perfectly.

Something that happened on baseball's opening day in 1954 illustrates the point well. The Milwaukee Braves and the Cincinnati Reds played each other, and a rookie for each team made his major-league debut during that game. The rookie who played for the Reds hit four doubles and helped his team win with a score of 9–8. The rookie for the Braves went 0 for 5. The Reds player was Jim Greengrass, a name you probably haven't heard. The other guy, who didn't get a hit, might be more familiar to you. His name was Hank Aaron, the player who became the best home-run hitter in the history of baseball.

If Aaron's expectations for that first game had been unrealistic, who knows? He might have given up baseball. Surely he wasn't happy about his performance that day, but he didn't think of himself as a failure. He had worked too hard for too long. He wasn't about to give up easily.

5. Achievers Focus on Strengths

Another way achievers keep themselves from personalizing failure is by focusing on their strengths. Bob Butera, former president of the New Jersey Devils hockey team, was asked what makes a winner. He answered, "What distinguishes winners from losers is that winners concentrate at all times on what they *can* do, not on what they can't do. If a guy is a great shooter but not a great skater, we tell him to think only about the shot, the shot, the shot—never about some other guy outskating him. The idea is to remember your successes."

If a weakness is a matter of character, it needs much attention. Focus on it until you shore it up. Otherwise, the best bet for failing forward is developing and maximizing your strengths.

6. Achievers Vary Approaches to Achievement

In *The Psychology of Achievement,* Brian Tracy writes about four millionaires who made their fortunes by age thirty-five. They were involved in an average of *seventeen* businesses before finding the one that took them to the top. They kept trying and changing until they found something that worked for them.

Achievers are willing to vary their approaches to problems. That's important in every walk of life, not just business. For example, if you're a fan of track-and-field events, you have undoubtedly enjoyed watching athletes compete in the high jump. I'm always amazed by the heights achieved by the men and women in that event. What's really interesting is that in the 1960s, the sport went through a major change in technique that allowed athletes to break the old records and push them up to new levels.

The person responsible for that change was Dick Fosbury. Where previous athletes used the straddle method to high jump, in which they went over the bar while facing it, with one arm and one leg leading, Fosbury developed a technique where he went over headfirst with his back to the bar. It was dubbed the Fosbury Flop.

Developing a new high jump technique was one thing. Getting it accepted by others was another matter. Fosbury remarked, "I was told over and over again that I would never be successful, that I was not going to be competitive and the technique was simply not going to work. All I could do was shrug and say, 'We'll just have to see.'"

And people did see. Fosbury won the gold medal in the Mexico City Olympics in 1968, shattering the previous Olympic record and setting a new world record in the process. Since then, nearly all world-class high jumpers use his technique. To achieve his goals, Fosbury varied his approach to high jumping, and he didn't allow others' comments to make him feel like a failure.

7. Achievers Bounce Back

All achievers have in common the ability to bounce back after an error, mistake, or failure. Psychologist Simone Caruthers says, "Life is a series of outcomes. Sometimes the outcome is what you want. Great. Figure out what you did right. Sometimes the outcome is what you don't want. Great. Figure out what you did so you don't do it again."[4] That's the key to bouncing back.

Achievers are able to keep moving forward no matter what happens. And that's made possible because they remember that failure does not make *them* failures. No one should take mistakes personally. That's the way to take yourself out of failure.

ONE WHO REFUSED TO BE A FAILURE

One of the best stories I've ever heard of someone who refused to take failure personally is that of Daniel "Rudy" Ruettiger, a kid who desperately wanted to play football for Notre Dame. You may have seen the film based on his life called *Rudy*. It was a good movie, but his real story is even more remarkable and compelling.

The first of fourteen children in a poor working-class family, Rudy loved sports as a kid and believed that might be his ticket out of Joliet, Illinois. In high school, he gave himself completely to football, but his heart was much greater than his physique. He was slow, and at five feet six inches tall and 190 pounds, he wasn't exactly built for the game.

RUDY'S DREAM

As a senior, he began dreaming about attending Notre Dame and playing football there. But Rudy faced another problem. His grades showed less promise than his physique. "I finished third in my class," he is fond of saying. "Not from the top, but from the bottom." He was a D student. He graduated from high school with a 1.77 grade point average.

For the next several years, Rudy changed his focus from one thing to another. He tried attending junior college for one semester but flunked every class. He went to work for two years at the local Commonwealth Edison power plant in Joliet—what he considered to be the ultimate dead-end job. And he even did a two-year hitch in the navy, which turned out to be a turning point for him. That's where he discovered that he wasn't dumb and that he could handle responsibility.

After his military service, he returned to Joliet and again worked in the power plant. He was more determined than ever to go to Notre Dame, despite the criticism of his family, friends, and coworkers. He knew he was not a failure, and he would find a way to go to South Bend.

MAKING A MOVE

If you saw the movie, then you know that Rudy eventually made it. He quit his job, moved to South Bend, and managed to get into Holy Cross College, a community college affiliated with the university. He attended the college for *two years* and earned a 4.0 average every semester before Notre Dame accepted him. He entered his dream school at age twenty-six—*eight years* after graduating from high school.

With two years of sports eligibility remaining, he went out for football. And he made the team as a scrub, one of the warm bodies they put in practice to keep the good players sharp. But Rudy made the most of it. He worked hard, and after a year, he went from the bottom of the scrubs all the way up to sixth string—the top of the scrubs. His last year, he worked hard again. And in the final game of his final season, Rudy lived his dream by getting to play.

RUDY'S LAST CHANCE

In the movie, Rudy Ruettiger gets in for only one play at the end of the game, and he sacks the quarterback. But that's not how it really happened.

"In real life, I had two chances to get the quarterback," says Rudy. "The first play, I didn't get there in time. I was too anxious and didn't execute the play. I failed." But once again, Rudy didn't let his failure make *him* a failure. He was determined to fail forward.

"I knew this was the last chance I would ever get," he explains. "When they snapped the ball, I wasn't worried about failing. I'd done that already, and I knew why I had failed. That's how you eliminate that fear. You keep learning until you have the confidence to perform when you have to . . . When they snapped the ball for the last time, I put the moves I'd rehearsed in my mind on the guy over me and I got the quarterback."

Overjoyed, the team carried him off the field in celebration. Rudy says it's the only time that's happened to a player in the history of Notre Dame football.

Today Rudy is a motivational speaker. And believe it or not, he was the force behind the making of the movie *Rudy*. Of course, it wasn't easy for him. It took him six years to see that happen. (Two years less than it took him to get to Notre Dame!)

The people in Hollywood told him, "You're not Paul Horning or Joe Montana." Rudy agreed.

"There's only one of them," he explained. "There's a million of me."[5]

And that's the great thing about Rudy's story. He doesn't have the athletic ability of Michael Jordan. Nor is he a genius like Mozart, Van Gogh, Edison, or Einstein. He's just a regular person—like you and me. The only reason he's an achiever instead of average is that he refused to let failure get the better of him. He learned that no matter how many times you fail, it doesn't have to make you a failure.

Your Third Step to Failing Forward:

Remove the "You" from Failure

If you've been thinking of yourself as a failure, you can break yourself out of that negative thinking pattern. Look at an area of your life where you have repeatedly failed, and do the following:

- *Examine your expectations for that area.* Write them down. Are they realistic? Do you expect to do everything perfectly? Do you expect to succeed on the first try? How many mistakes should you expect to make before you succeed? Adjust your expectations.

- *Find new ways to do your work.* Brainstorm at least twenty new approaches, and then try at least half of them.

- *Focus on your strengths.* How can you use your best skills and personal strengths to maximize your effort?

- *Vow to bounce back.* No matter how many times you fall down, pick yourself up and keep going.

Don't wait until you feel positive to move forward. Act your way into feeling good. That's the only way to start thinking more positively about yourself.

Steps to Failing Forward:

1. Realize there is one major difference between average people and achieving people.

2. Learn a new definition of *failure.*

3. Remove the "you" from failure.

4

You're Too Old to Cry, but
It Hurts Too Much to Laugh

Fear makes come true that which one is afraid of.
—VIKTOR FRANKL

Just about everyone has heard of the Wright brothers, the bicycle mechanics who pioneered manned motorized flight in the first part of the twentieth century. The circumstances surrounding Orville and Wilbur Wright's first flight on December 17, 1903, make an interesting story. (It's certainly a story that illustrates how to fail forward.) But what you may not know is that prior to that day, the Wrights, unknowns with no university education, were not the leaders in aviation. They were obscure at best, and another man was expected to put the first airplane in the air.

His name was Dr. Samuel P. Langley. He was a respected former professor of mathematics and astronomy who at that time was the director of the Smithsonian Institution. Langley was an accomplished thinker, scientist, and inventor. He had published several important works on aerodynamics, and he possessed a vision for achieving manned flight. In fact, in the mid- to late 1890s, he had done extensive experiments with large unmanned plane models and had achieved a high degree of success.

COMMISSIONED TO SUCCEED

In 1898, Langley approached the U.S. War Department for funding to design and build an airplane to carry a man aloft. And the department gave him a commission of $50,000—a huge sum at that time. Langley went right to work. By 1901, he had successfully tested an unmanned gasoline-powered heavier-than-air craft: It was the first in history. And when he enlisted the aid of Charles Manley, an engineer who built a powerful new lightweight engine based on the designs of Stephen Balzar, his success seemed inevitable.

On October 8, 1903, Langley expected his years of work to come to fruition. As journalists and curious onlookers watched, Charles Manley, wearing a cork-lined jacket, strode across the deck of a modified houseboat and climbed into the pilot's seat of a craft called the *Great Aerodrome*. The full-sized, motorized device was perched atop a specially built catapult designed to initiate the *Aerodrome*'s flight into the air. But when they attempted the launch, part of the *Aerodrome* got caught, and the biplane was flung into sixteen feet of water a mere fifty yards away from the boat.

Criticism of Langley was brutal. For example, read this report in the *New York Times:*

> The ridiculous fiasco which attended the attempt at aerial navigation in the Langley flying machine was not unexpected. The flying machine which will really fly might be evolved by the combined and continuous efforts of mathematicians and mechanicians [sic] in from one to ten million years . . . No doubt the problem has its attractions for those it interests, but to ordinary men, it would seem as if the effort might be employed more profitably.[1]

IN THE FACE OF FAILURE

At first, Langley didn't let that failure or the accompanying criticism deter him. Eight weeks later in early December, he and Manley were ready to attempt flight again. They had made numerous modifications to the *Aerodrome*, and once more Manley climbed into the cockpit from the houseboat's deck, ready to make history. But as before, disaster struck. This time the cable supports to the wings snapped as the plane was launched, the craft caught again on the launch rail, and it plunged into the river upside down. Manley nearly died.

Again the criticism was fierce. His *Great Aerodrome* was called "Langley's Folly," and Langley himself was accused of wasting public funds. The *New York Times* commented, "We hope that Prof. Langley will not put his substantial greatness as a scientist in further peril by continuing to waste his time, and the money involved, in further airship experiments."[2] He didn't.

Langley said afterward, "I have brought to a close the portion of the work which seemed to be specially mine. The demonstration of the practicality of mechanical flight. For the next stage, which is the commercial and practical development of the idea, it is probable that the world may look to others." In other words, Langley had given up. Defeated and demoralized, he had abandoned his decades-long pursuit of flight without ever having seen one of his planes piloted to success. Just days later, Orville and Wilbur Wright—uneducated, unknown, and unfunded—flew their plane "Flyer I" over the sand dunes of Kitty Hawk, North Carolina.

Two Perspectives

Author J. I. Packer states, "A moment of conscious triumph makes one feel that after this nothing will really matter; a moment of realized disaster makes one feel that this is the end of everything. But neither feeling is realistic, for neither event is really what it is felt to be."

The Wright brothers did not rest on their success. The rush of achievement that day in December of 1903 did not make them think they had arrived. They continued experimenting and working, and eventually the public acknowledged their achievements. In contrast, Langley let his moment of disaster make him think it was the end. He abandoned his experiments. Two years later he suffered a stroke, and a year after that he died. And today, while even young schoolchildren have heard of the Wright brothers, Langley is remembered only by relatively few aviation buffs.

WHEN FAILURE GETS YOU BY THE HEART

What happened in the life of Samuel Langley occurs in the lives of too many people today. They allow failure to get the better of them emotionally, and it stops them from achieving their dreams.

Let's face it. Failure can be very painful—sometimes physically and more often emotionally. Seeing part of your vision fall flat really hurts. And if people heap ridicule on top of your hurt feelings, you feel even worse. *The first important step in weathering failure is learning not to personalize it—making sure you know that your failure does not make* you *a failure.* But there's more to it than that. For many people the pain of failure leads to fear of failure. And they become like the person who says, "I'm too old to cry, but it hurts too much to laugh." That's when many people get stuck in the fear cycle. And if fear overcomes you, it's almost impossible to fail forward.

> *The first important step in weathering failure is learning not to personalize it.*

A CYCLE YOU DON'T WANT TO RIDE

Take a look at what typically happens to someone who is unable to overcome the fear of failure and gets caught in the fear cycle.

Prior negative experiences cause the person to develop a fear of failure that starts the cycle. For example, let's say someone experienced failure as a child trying to sell candy door-to-door to raise money for school. Later

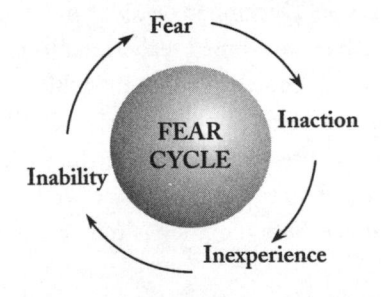

as an adult, he is put in a situation that seems similar, and fear strikes. Whether he is a salesperson with a need to make calls on customers or a pastor with a mission to visit people in their homes, that old childhood failure may generate fear. The fear of rejection creates inaction. Because the person doesn't act, he doesn't gain personal experience in that situation—which is the key to learning and overcoming future obstacles. The lack of experience breeds an inability to handle similar situations. And that ultimately feeds and increases the fear. The longer the fear remains unchecked, the harder a person has to work to break the cycle.

FEAR OF FAILURE STOPS FORWARD PROGRESS

The inaction that results when people are stuck in the fear cycle takes on many forms. Here are the three most common ones I've observed:

1. Paralysis

For some people, fear of failure brings about absolute paralysis. They stop trying to do anything that might lead to failure. President Harry S. Truman offered this opinion: "The worst danger we face is the danger of being paralyzed by doubts and fears. This danger is brought on by those who abandon faith and sneer at hope. It is brought on by those who spread cynicism and distrust and try to blind us to the great chance to do good for all mankind." People whose fear paralyzes them give up any hope of moving forward.

2. Procrastination

Other people maintain the hope of progress but never get around to following through. Someone once called procrastination the fertilizer that makes difficulties grow. Victor Kiam stated it even more strongly; he called it opportunity's natural assassin.

Procrastination steals a person's time, productivity, and potential. As President John F. Kennedy said, "There are risks and costs to a program of action, but they are far less than the long-range risks and costs of comfortable inaction." Procrastination is too high a price to pay for fear of failure.

3. *Purposelessness*

Tom Peters, coauthor of *In Search of Excellence,* emphasizes that there's nothing more useless than someone who comes to the end of the day and congratulates himself, saying, "Well, I made it through the day without screwing up." Yet that's what many people who fear failure do. Rather than pursue worthy objectives, they avoid the pain of making mistakes. And in the midst of that transition, they lose sight of any sense of purpose that they might have once possessed.

As fear of failure and the resulting inactivity compound, a person in the fear cycle exhibits additional negative side effects:

- *Self-pity.* He feels sorry for himself. And as time goes on, he takes less responsibility for his inactivity and starts thinking of himself as a victim.

- *Excuses.* A person can fall down many times, but he won't be a failure until he says that somebody pushed him. In fact, the person who makes a mistake, then offers an excuse for it, adds a second mistake to his first. A person can break out of the fear cycle only by taking personal responsibility for his inaction.

- *Misused energy.* Constant fear divides the mind and causes a person to lose focus. If he is going in too many directions at once, he doesn't get anywhere. It's comparable to stomping the gas pedal of a car that's in neutral.

- *Hopelessness.* If allowed to run their course, continual fear and inaction rob a person of hope. And poet Henry Wadsworth Longfellow described the situation in this way: "The setting of a great hope is like the setting of the sun. The brightness of our life is gone."

BREAKING THE CYCLE

People who want to get out of the fear cycle often spend time feeling guilty for their inability to change. But one of the reasons they are stuck in the fear cycle is that they focus their energy on the wrong part of the cycle. Since they know that fear got the cycle going, they believe that they have to eliminate it to break the cycle. Yet most people are unable to do that. You can't avoid fear. No magic potion will take it away. And you can't wait for motivation to get you going. To conquer fear, you have to feel the fear and take action anyway.

Several years ago while I was sitting in my doctor's waiting room, I came across a few paragraphs in a medical magazine that describe the battle to act:

We hear it almost every day: sigh, sigh, sigh.

I just can't get myself motivated to . . . [lose weight, test my blood sugar, etc.]. And we hear an equal number of sighs from diabetes educators who can't get their patients motivated to do the right things for their diabetes and health.

We have news for you. Motivation is not going to strike you like lightning. And motivation is not something that someone else—nurse, doctor, family member—can bestow or force on you. The whole idea of motivation is a trap. Forget motivation. Just *do it*. Exercise, lose weight, test your blood sugar, or whatever. Do it without motivation and then guess what. After you start doing the thing, that's when the motivation comes and makes it easy for you to keep on doing it.

Motivation is like love and happiness. It's a by-product. When you're actively engaged in doing something, it sneaks up and zaps you when you least expect it.

As Harvard psychologist Jerome Bruner says, "You're more likely to act yourself into feeling than feel yourself into action." So act! Whatever it is you know you should do, do it.

GET MOVING, BUILD MOMENTUM, MAKE MISTAKES, MOVE ON

Playwright George Bernard Shaw asserted, "A life spent in making mistakes is not only more honorable but more useful than a life spent doing nothing." To overcome fear and break the cycle, you have to be willing to recognize that you will spend much of your life making mistakes. The bad news is that if you've been inactive for a long time, getting started is hard to do. The good news is that as soon as you start moving, it gets easier.

If you can take action and keep making mistakes, you gain experience. (That's why President Theodore Roosevelt said, "He who makes no mistakes makes no progress.") That experience eventually brings competence, and you make fewer mistakes. As a result, your fear becomes less paralyzing. But the whole cycle-breaking process starts with action. You must act your way into feeling, not wait for positive emotions to carry you forward.

> *You're more likely to act yourself into feeling than feel yourself into action.*
> —*JEROME BRUNER*

An African parable captures the idea very well:

Every morning in Africa, a gazelle wakes up. It knows that it must run faster than the fastest lion or it will be killed. Every morning a lion wakes up. It knows that it must outrun the slowest gazelle or it will starve to death.

It doesn't matter whether you are a lion or a gazelle: When the sun comes up you had better be running.

If you have always had a hard time failing forward, then you have to get yourself moving. It doesn't matter what has stopped you or how long you have been inactive. The only way to break the cycle is to face your fear and take action, even though it may seem small or insignificant.

EVEN THE BEST GET STUCK SOMETIMES

Many unsuccessful people get stuck in the fear cycle. But the same thing happens to high achievers. For example, when you look at the life of the composer George Frederick Handel, you see a successful person who found himself in a rut that he needed desperately to break out of.

Handel was a musical prodigy. Though his father wanted him to study law, he gravitated to music at an early age. By age seventeen, he held the post of church organist at the cathedral in Halle, his hometown. A year later, he became a violinist and harpsichordist at the kaiser's opera house in Hamburg. By age twenty-one, he was a keyboard virtuoso. When he turned to composing, he gained immediate fame and soon was appointed Kapellmeister conductor to the elector of Hanover (later King George I of England). When he moved to England, his renown grew. By the time he was forty, he was world famous.

A REVERSAL OF FORTUNE

Despite Handel's talent and fame, he faced considerable adversity. Competition with rival English composers was fierce. Audiences were fickle and sometimes didn't turn out for his performances. And he was frequently the victim of the changing political winds of the times. Several times he found himself penniless and on the verge of bankruptcy. The pain of rejection and failure was difficult to bear, especially following his previous success.

Then his problems were compounded by failing health. He suffered a seizure or stroke, which left his right arm limp and caused him to lose the use of four fingers on his right hand. Although he recovered, he remained despondent. In 1741, Handel decided that it was time to retire, even though he was only fifty-six. He was discouraged, miserable, and consumed with debt. He felt certain he would land in debtors' prison. On April 8, he gave what he considered his farewell concert. Disappointed and filled with self-pity, he gave up.

THE INSPIRATION TO MOVE FORWARD

But in August of that year, something incredible happened. A wealthy friend named Charles Jennings visited Handel and gave him a libretto based on the life of Christ. The work intrigued Handel—enough to stir him to action. He began writing. And immediately the floodgates of inspiration opened in him. His cycle of inactivity was broken. For twenty-one days, he wrote almost nonstop. Then he spent another two days creating the orchestrations. In twenty-four days, he had completed the 260-page manuscript. He called the piece *Messiah*.

Today, Handel's *Messiah* is considered a masterpiece and the culmination of the composer's work. In fact, Sir Newman Flower, one of Handel's biographers, said of the writing of *Messiah*, "Considering the immensity of the work, and the short time involved, it will remain, perhaps forever, the greatest feat in the whole history of music composition."[3]

When it comes to getting over the emotional hurts of failure, it really doesn't matter how good or bad your personal history is. The only thing that matters is that you face your fear and get moving. Do that, and you give yourself the opportunity to learn how to fail forward.

Your Fourth Step to Failing Forward:
Take Action and Reduce Your Fear

What objective essential to your success are you most afraid of tackling right now? Write what it is here:

The only way to get going is to face that fear and act. Write down all your fears associated with the activity:

Examine your list and accept the fact that you are afraid. Determine what *first step* you can take to get started on achieving that objective. It doesn't matter whether it's small or large. Just do it. If you fail at it, do it again. Keep trying until you accomplish that first step. Then figure out what the next step is.

Remember, it's almost impossible to feel your way into acting. You must act your way into feeling. The only way to get over the fear is to take action.

Steps to Failing Forward:

1. Realize there is one major difference between average people and achieving people.

2. Learn a new definition of *failure*.

3. Remove the "you" from failure.

4. Take action and reduce your fear.

5

Find the Exit Off the Failure Freeway

The moment a question comes to your mind, see yourself mentally taking hold of it and disposing of it. In that moment is your choice made. Thus you learn to take the path to the right. Thus you learn to become the decider and not the vacillator. Thus you build character.

—H. VAN ANDERSON

Business professors Gary Hamel and C. K. Prahalad have written about an experiment that was conducted with a group of monkeys. It is a vivid story of failure.

Four monkeys were placed in a room that had a tall pole in the center. Suspended from the top of that pole was a bunch of bananas. One of the hungry monkeys started climbing the pole to get something to eat, but just as he reached out to grab a banana, he was doused with a torrent of cold water. Squealing, he scampered down the pole and abandoned his attempt to feed himself. Each monkey made a similar attempt, and each one was drenched with cold water. After making several attempts, they finally gave up.

Then researchers removed one of the monkeys from the room and replaced him with a new monkey. As the newcomer began to climb the pole, the other three grabbed him and pulled him down to the ground.

47

After trying to climb the pole several times and being dragged down by the others, he finally gave up and never attempted to climb the pole again.

The researchers replaced the original monkeys, one by one, and each time a new monkey was brought in, he would be dragged down by the others before he could reach the bananas. In time, the room was filled with monkeys who had never received a cold shower. None of them would climb the pole, but not one of them knew why.[1]

DON'T LET FAILURE MAKE A MONKEY OUT OF YOU

Unfortunately people who have gotten used to failure can be a lot like those monkeys. They make the same mistakes again and again, yet they are never quite sure why. And as a result, they never seem to get off what I call the failure freeway. The old saying is true: If you always do what you've always done, then you will always get what you've always gotten.

> *If you always do what you've always done, then you will always get what you've always gotten.*

Let's face it. People are prone to ruts. And anyone who has been conditioned to think failure is his fate has an especially hard time exiting the failure freeway. If you feel like one of the monkeys in the experiment—meaning you can't seem to achieve what you desire but you don't know why—then take a look at the pattern many failure-prone people fall into and the ultimate solution.

IT ALL STARTS WITH A *MESS UP*

What starts people down the failure freeway is a common mistake, failure, or mess up. But people who stay on the failure freeway don't think that it's their fault. They are similar to the drivers who wrote the following explanations for the auto accidents in which they were involved:

- "As I reached an intersection, a hedge sprang up, obscuring my vision."

- "An invisible car came out of nowhere, struck my car, and vanished."

- "The telephone pole was approaching fast. I attempted to swerve out of its path when it struck my front end."

- "The indirect cause of this accident was a little guy in a small car with a big mouth."

- "I had been driving my car for four years when I fell asleep at the wheel and had an accident."

- "I was on the way to the doctor's with rear-end trouble when my universal joint gave way, causing me to have an accident."

- "To avoid hitting the bumper of the car in front, I struck the pedestrian."

- "I was coming home, pulled into the wrong driveway, and hit a tree I did not have."

- "I was just keeping up with the cars behind me."

- "The pedestrian had no idea which direction to run, so I ran over him."

- "The guy was all over the road, and I had to swerve a number of times before hitting him."

- "I pulled away at the side of the road, glanced at my mother-in-law, and headed over the embankment."

Many people on the failure freeway make mistakes but refuse to admit them. They see every obstacle or error as somebody else's fault. And as a result, they generally respond in one or more of the following ways:

Blow Up

One reaction to failure that keeps people driving on the failure freeway is anger. You've probably seen it. People make a minor mistake and angrily overreact to it, taking out their frustration on themselves or others around them.

Unchecked anger makes a small problem bigger. Nineteenth-century

English author Charles Buxton summed it up: "Bad temper is its own scourge. Few things are more bitter than to feel bitter. A man's venom poisons himself more than his victim." If a person doesn't govern his temper, it will govern him.

Cover Up

It's in the nature of people to try to cover up their mistakes. That tendency is as old as Adam and Eve in the Garden of Eden—and it's usually just as successful for us today as it was for them.

I heard a joke about a young navy pilot on maneuvers that shows how people often react to their mistakes. Prior to takeoff, the commanding admiral had ordered absolute radio silence from everyone engaged in the exercise. But one pilot mistakenly turned on his radio and was heard to mutter, "Boy, am I fouled up!"

> *Don't waste energy trying to cover up failure. Learn from your failures and go on to the next challenge. It's okay to fail. If you're not failing, you're not growing.*
>
> —H. STANLEY JUDD

The admiral grabbed the mike from a radio operator and said, "Will the pilot who broke the radio silence identify himself immediately!"

There was a long silence, and then a voice was heard over the radio: "I may be fouled up, but I'm not *that* fouled up!"

People's desire to make sure others don't see their mistakes isn't always so humorous. For example, take the case of Nicholas Leeson. In 1995, the twenty-eight-year-old worked for the British bank Barings. He controlled huge amounts of money for the organization, which he tried to increase through what's been called casino-style investing. When Leeson's dealings resulted in huge losses, he covered them up and made even riskier trades to try to recoup his losses. Analysts said it was like betting double or nothing in a gambling game. The problem was that Leeson kept coming up with nothing, creating bigger and bigger losses. Ultimately his actions cost

Barings $1.3 *billion*. He single-handedly put one of the oldest banks in the world out of business.

H. Stanley Judd said, "Don't waste energy trying to cover up failure. Learn from your failures and go on to the next challenge. It's okay to fail. If you're not failing, you're not growing." Anyone who wants to get off the failure freeway needs to 'fess up rather than cover up.

Speed Up

Particularly stubborn people sometimes try to leave their troubles behind by working harder and faster, but without changing their direction. They're like the person trying to get the square peg in the round hole who first tries to place the peg in the hole, then tries to shove it in, then takes a hammer and tries to pound it in. They're working hard but getting nowhere.

William Dean Singleton, co-owner of MediaNews Group Inc., addresses this tendency: "Too many people, when they make a mistake, just keep stubbornly plowing ahead and end up repeating the same mistakes. I believe in the motto, 'Try and try again.' But the way I read it, it says, 'Try, then stop and think. Then try again.'"

> *Too many people, when they make a mistake, just keep stubbornly plowing ahead and end up repeating the same mistakes. I believe in the motto, "Try and try again." But the way I read it, it says, "Try, then stop and think. Then try again."*
>
> —WILLIAM DEAN SINGLETON

Back Up

Have you ever been talking with someone who made a thoughtless remark during a conversation, and as soon as he said it, you could tell he knew he had made a mistake? Yet when you called him on it, he refused to admit it. No matter what you said, he kept backing up and trying to justify the remark, which made him look sillier and sillier. That's what people who back up do. And if they make a habit of it, they get stuck on the failure freeway.

When my wife, Margaret, and I were raising our children, Elizabeth and Joel Porter (both of whom are now married), we found that our son had a mind and will of his own. When he did something wrong, his first move was to lie. Then he'd back up and try to cover it up. I can still picture his offended expression as he emphatically denied having eaten the chocolate candy—with his nine-year-old face smeared with chocolate. Margaret and I worked very hard to break him of that inclination.

> *Ninety percent of all those who fail are not actually defeated. They simply quit.*
>
> —PAUL J. MEYER

General Peyton C. March perceived, "Any man worth his salt will stick up for what he believes right, but it takes a slightly bigger man to acknowledge instantly and without reservation that he is in error." I'm relieved that today my boy Joel is a man, and when he's wrong, he admits it. And that's good because nobody can exit off the failure freeway if he keeps backing up.

Give Up

If you stay on the failure freeway long enough, you eventually *slow up*. It's similar to what happens on the Interstate 285 loop around my hometown of Atlanta at rush hour—gridlock. And that's when a lot of people simply *give up*. Personal growth expert Paul J. Meyer says, "Ninety percent of all those who fail are not actually defeated. They simply quit."

BUT TO FAIL FORWARD, YOU'VE GOT TO *WAKE UP*

There's really only one solution to the gridlock on the failure freeway, and that's to wake up and find the exit. To leave the road of continual failure, a person must first utter the three most difficult words to say: "I was wrong." He has to open his eyes, admit his mistakes, and accept complete responsibility for his current wrong actions and attitudes. Every failure you experience is a fork in the road. It's an opportunity to take the right action, learn from your mistakes, and begin again.

Leadership expert Peter Drucker says, "The better a man is, the more mistakes he will make, for the more new things he will try. I would never promote to a top-level job a man who was not making mistakes . . . otherwise he is sure to be mediocre." Mistakes really do pave the road to achievement.

Here is an acrostic I created to help me keep mistakes in perspective. Mistakes are . . .

> *M*essages that give us feedback about life.
> *I*nterruptions that should cause us to reflect and think.
> *S*ignposts that direct us to the right path.
> *T*ests that push us toward greater maturity.
> *A*wakenings that keep us in the game mentally.
> *K*eys that we can use to unlock the next door of opportunity.
> *E*xplorations that let us journey where we've never been before.
> *S*tatements about our development and progress.

A few years ago as I spoke at an event attended by more than fifty thousand people, I shared something written by Portia Nelson. It has been one of the most-requested pieces by people who have heard me speak. It's called "Autobiography in Five Short Chapters." Better than almost anything else, it describes the process of exiting the failure freeway:

Chapter 1. I walk down the street. There is a deep hole in the sidewalk. I fall in. I am lost. I am helpless. It isn't my fault. It takes forever to find a way out.

Chapter 2. I walk down the street. There is a deep hole in the sidewalk. I pretend I don't see it. I fall in again. I can't believe I am in the same place, but it isn't my fault. It still takes a long time to get out.

Chapter 3. I walk down the same street. There is a deep hole in the sidewalk. I see it is there. I still fall in. It's a habit. My eyes are open. I know where I am. It is my fault. I get out immediately.

Chapter 4. I walk down the same street. There is a deep hole in the sidewalk. I walk around it.

Chapter 5. I walk down another street.

The only way to exit the failure freeway and see the new territory of achievement is to take full responsibility for yourself and your mistakes. Michael Korda, editor in chief of Simon and Schuster, declared, "Success on any major scale requires you to accept responsibility . . . In the final analysis, the one quality that all successful people have is the ability to take on responsibility."

> *Success on any major scale requires you to accept responsibility . . . In the final analysis, the one quality that all successful people have is the ability to take on responsibility.*
>
> *—MICHAEL KORDA*

YOUR MOST IMPORTANT ABILITY: RESPONSIBILITY

The fight to take responsibility occurs within. And rarely does talent, intelligence, or opportunity make the difference in whether a person wins that battle. It calls for character. That's why Stewart B. Johnson remarked, "Our business in life is not to get ahead of others, but to get ahead of ourselves—to break our own records, to outstrip our yesterday by our today."

You can tell when people develop deeper character, accept responsibility for themselves, and begin learning from their failures. It really shows in their performance. For example, I observed that in Chris Chandler of the NFL's Atlanta Falcons after I moved to Georgia.

Chandler is a quarterback who had a history of floating from team to team. Prior to his employment with Atlanta, he had played for five teams in nine years, and he had never excelled. But everything started to change for him in Phoenix. That's where he met Jerry Rhome.

"I was at a point where I really didn't care anymore," says Chandler about that part of his career. His view of the league affected his willingness to take full responsibility for his lack of success. "I thought the NFL was just totally political, and I was ready to quit. Jerry brought back my competitiveness, and he taught me how to play. He made it fun again."

How did Rhome accomplish that? He told Chandler the truth. "I told him after the season that he had a lot of ability, but he was uncoachable," said Rhome, "and I offered to work with him."[2]

At first Chandler resisted. He expected everyone else to adjust to his style and ability. But then he changed his mind and accepted Rhome's offer. With help, hard work, and a new willingness to change himself rather than expecting others to change, Chandler has become one of the best quarterbacks in the NFL, taking his team to the Super Bowl in 1999.

ANOTHER ROAD TO FAME

Not everyone learns the lesson of accepting responsibility for her actions. One of the most unusual stories I've ever encountered about someone on the failure freeway is that of Rosie Ruiz. Back in 1980, she was the first woman to cross the finish line of the Boston Marathon with the third-fastest women's time ever. But from the moment that she finished the race, people were suspicious of her "victory."

The person most shocked was Jacqueline Gareau. Though not favored to win the race, Gareau had been training to run it for three years. And during the course of the race, she had pulled ahead of all the other women. It appeared that she was going to win. But about a mile from the finish line, another woman suddenly appeared running ahead of her. And that other woman—Ruiz—finished before her and was declared the women's winner.

Immediately there was a stir.

"I knew something was fishy," said men's winner Bill Rodgers. He said that Ruiz had too much body fat and not enough muscle to be a distance runner. On top of that, at the finish line she didn't appear fatigued, wasn't sweating heavily, and displayed unfamiliarity with running terminology while being interviewed.

The race officials were suspicious, and they began to investigate. They found that Ruiz had qualified for the Boston Marathon by obtaining a fraudulent qualifying finish for the New York Marathon. They surmised that in the Boston race, Ruiz had jumped into a group of runners a mile from the finish line, never suspecting that she was actually ahead of all the other women. The Boston Athletic Association disqualified her, and a week later, they awarded Gareau the winner's medal.

STILL ON THE FREEWAY

What's most amazing is that even years later, Ruiz still hadn't learned from her mistake. At a ten-kilometer race in Miami, Gareau saw Ruiz and tried to talk to her to clear the air. Gareau recounted: "I said, 'Why did you do that in Boston?' And she said, 'Oh, I did run it.' So, there's no way you're going to have a conversation with her."

Two years after her appearance in the Boston Marathon, Ruiz was arrested and charged with stealing cash and checks from her employer. A year later she was convicted for trying to sell two kilos of cocaine to an undercover police officer.[3] As Sir Josiah Stamp said, "It is easy to dodge our responsibilities, but we cannot dodge the consequences of our responsibilities."

> *It is easy to dodge our responsibilities, but we cannot dodge the consequences of our responsibilities.*
>
> —SIR JOSIAH STAMP

I don't know what Rosie Ruiz is doing today. Her past activities remind me of the bumper sticker I've seen that says, "Don't follow me. I'm lost." Back then, Ruiz was doing a lot of moving, but she wasn't getting anywhere. Let's hope she's finally found the exit off the failure freeway.

Your Fifth Step to Failing Forward:

Change Your Response to Failure by Accepting Responsibility

Take a hard look at a very recent failure that you have considered not to be your fault. Look for *anything* negative in the failure that you should claim responsibility for. Then own it.

Once you begin thinking in terms of what *is* your responsibility, you will be able to change. And changing your mind—the way you think about failure—is the next step to failing forward and the subject of the next part of the book.

Steps to Failing Forward:

1. Realize there is one major difference between average people and achieving people.

2. Learn a new definition of *failure*.

3. Remove the "you" from failure.

4. Take action and reduce your fear.

5. Change your response to failure by accepting responsibility.

Do You Mind Changing Your Mind?

6

No Matter What Happens to You, Failure Is an Inside Job

Life is not simply holding a good hand.
Life is playing a poor hand well.

—*Danish saying*

When you learn to accept responsibility for yourself, your problems, and your failures, you are better prepared to fail forward. But what about when you're faced with overwhelming difficulties that you didn't create and you can't control?

At no time in life are people more prone to allow failure to overcome them and to give up than when external circumstances cause extreme hardship or grief. But ultimately no matter whether the difficulty is self-created or comes from somewhere outside them, *failure* is created *within* them. It is always an inside job. Let me illustrate.

In the spring of 1999, my publisher, Thomas Nelson, invited me to speak at various cities around the country on a book tour. One of my stops on that trip was in Lexington, Kentucky, and it was there that I met Greg Horn, owner of the Payless Food Center, a grocery store in Cynthiana, Kentucky. Greg told me an incredible story that shows that no matter what happens *to* you, the important thing is what happens *in* you.

Keeping His Head (and Heart) Above Water

On March 1, 1997, Greg was in Bossier City, Louisiana, where he had traveled from his home in Kentucky to attend my two-day leadership conference. When the conference was over, he boarded a plane and headed to St. Louis on the first leg of his journey home, excitedly considering how to put into action the leadership training he had received.

When he got to the gate in St. Louis for his connecting flight to Lexington, he was surprised to discover that it had been delayed because of bad weather in Kentucky. When that delay turned into a canceled flight, Greg was stuck in St. Louis overnight. He didn't think too much of it. He was a seasoned traveler and had learned to roll with the punches when on the road. And the next morning, he caught the first flight out.

Only when he landed in Lexington did he realize the magnitude of the problems caused by the weather. As he drove north from the airport toward Cynthiana, he started to see the effects of the heavy rain that had canceled his flight. When he learned that the Licking River, which flowed through Cynthiana, had flooded its banks, he started to worry about his store. He headed straight for it, wanting to make sure everything was all right. The thirty-mile trip seemed to take forever.

And the Bad News Is . . .

When Greg finally arrived, he found the area flooded. Standing two hundred yards away from his store, he could see only its roof and the sign: Payless Food Center. The rest was under water. Demoralized, he headed for home, but he couldn't get anywhere near his house either.

For three days Greg stayed with his sister in Lexington, waiting for the water to subside and wondering what he was going to do. That's when he called his insurance agent and discovered news that made things even worse: He had every kind of insurance except—you guessed it—flood coverage. There would be no financial relief.

WEIGHING THE DAMAGE

All in all, five days passed before Greg could get into the store. And when he opened the doors, he faced complete devastation. He stood in the midst of $500,000 worth of waterlogged, spoiled inventory. His electronic cash registers were full of filthy water, and a huge five-hundred-pound freezer that usually held bags of ice had been lifted by the floodwaters and dumped on top of a checkout stand. It was the kind of demoralizing mess that makes a person want to lock the doors and walk away forever.

"At that point I had a choice," says Greg. He could have given up, acknowledging that tragedy had caused his business to fail. "I could have filed for bankruptcy. But I didn't want to do that. That's when the principles that I had learned a few days earlier at the leadership conference came back to me: It's not what happens *to* me; it's what happens *in* me. It's not the size of the problem, but how I handle the problem. When I fall, keep getting up. I was determined to overcome this experience," adds Greg.

He assessed that the building was still structurally solid, but the interior of the store was trashed. Everything inside had to be removed by hand. It took twenty-two truckloads to haul off the ruined inventory. All the cash registers had to be replaced. So did the tile floor. He and his staff worked feverishly around the clock. It cost Greg $1 million to do it, but he was able to reopen his Payless Food Center—and he did it in a miraculous sixteen days. The store was closed for only twenty-one days after the flood.

ASSESSING THE IMPACT

How does a person assess the impact of an event like the flood that ruined Greg Horn's store? You can measure it in dollars. You can measure it in days. You can gauge the emotional impact on the owner. But Greg would encourage you to measure it in the lives of other people: "Being able to reopen in only twenty-one days allowed eighty people to return to work, many of whom were personally affected by the flood. And as it says in Proverbs, 'Humility comes before honor.'"

Greg Horn is a great example of a person who learned how to fail forward. Many people desire to control the circumstances of their lives, but the truth is that we cannot determine what will come our way. We can't control the hands we're dealt, only how we play the cards. That's what Greg did. He could have made the flood a tombstone for his store and his career. Instead, he turned it into a stepping-stone—for his employees, his community, and himself.

"I got into the grocery business because I wanted to make an impact on people," says Greg. "Before I opened the store in Cynthiana, I worked for Hershey's Chocolate and had a $1.2 million territory. I was making a good living, but that wasn't enough."

Since the time of the flood, he has received numerous awards and has been recognized as the businessperson of the year by his local chamber of commerce. And he is using the negative experience of the flood to begin a career in motivational speaking. Almost every week Greg publicly communicates his message of encouragement to others.[1]

South African general Jan Christiaan Smuts declared, "A man is not defeated by his opponents but by himself." That's true. No matter how daunting the circumstances of your life may be, the greatest battle you wage against failure occurs on the inside, not the outside. How do you fight that battle? You start by cultivating the right attitude.

> *A man is not defeated by his opponents but by himself.*
> —JAN CHRISTIAAN SMUTS

HOW YOU SEE IS WHAT YOU GET

You're probably familiar with Murphy's Law, which says, "If anything bad can happen, it will—and at the worst possible time." And then there's the Peter Principle, which says, "People always rise to the level of their incompetence." (By the way, both were written by pessimists!) A similar saying is the law of human behavior: "Sooner or later we get just what we expect."

I have a question to ask you: Is the law of human behavior optimistic or pessimistic? Stop and think about your answer. I say that because your response reveals your attitude. If you expect the worst out of life, then you probably said the law was written by a pessimist. If you have a positive outlook, then you probably answered "optimist" because the prospect of getting what you expect is encouraging to you. Your attitude determines your outlook.

POSITIVE ATTITUDE: THE FIRST KEY TO WHAT HAPPENS IN YOU

The first element in winning the internal battle against failure is a positive outlook. University of Pennsylvania psychology professor Martin Seligman, who has studied employees in thirty different industries, observes, "The people who bounce back are optimists."[2]

Let's face it. Not everyone is naturally optimistic. Some people are born seeing the glass half empty rather than half full. But no matter what your natural bent is, you can become a more optimistic person. How do you cultivate optimism? By learning the secret of contentment. If you can learn that, then no matter what happens to you, you can weather the storm and build on the good you find in any situation.

Contentment. That's not a popular concept these days. One reason is that our culture actually discourages the idea of contentment. People are continually bombarded with the message, "What you have isn't enough. You need more—a bigger house, a better car, a larger salary, whiter teeth, sweeter breath, nicer clothes . . ." The list is endless. But the truth is that possessing healthy contentment is essential to being able to withstand failure.

There are a lot of misconceptions about contentment. Let's look at what it's *not:*

1. *Not* Containing *Your Emotions*

We all experience negative emotions. How do you think Greg Horn felt when he saw his store six feet under water? Although you don't want to let your emotions run amok, you shouldn't try to stuff them either. Denial doesn't help you become content. Your emotions will come out eventually, even if you try to bury them.

If you try suppressing your emotions as a strategy for attaining contentment, you might end up like the older man who lay in the hospital on the verge of death. As he floated on the verge of consciousness for two weeks, his faithful wife sat in a chair by him every moment. When he finally became lucid enough to speak, he whispered, "Honey, you have been with me through all the bad times. When I got fired, you were there to support me. When we lost the house, you never left my side. You were there when I lost the business, and when my health started failing."

"Yes, dear," she answered, smiling.

"You know what?" he said.

"What, dear?" she asked.

"You're bad luck!"

Stuffing your emotions will not lead to contentment.

2. *Not* Maintaining *Your Current Situation*

My dad, who was a pastor for many years, used to tell the story about a farmer in one of his churches who refused to improve himself. Dad would try to encourage and cajole him, but he said the man just wouldn't change. His response to my father was always the same: "I'm not making much progress, but I'm well established."

One day my father was driving past that man's farm, and he saw that the farmer's tractor was stuck in the mud. No matter what the man did, mud flew, and the tractor stayed put.

After the farmer gave it one more try and was no better off than he had been before, he started cussing up a storm. At that point, my dad rolled down his window and hollered out to the man, "Well, you're not making much progress, but you certainly are well established."

Being content doesn't mean being satisfied with a bad situation. It simply means having a good attitude as you work your way out of it. When Greg Horn found his store flooded, he didn't give up, and he didn't give in. He made the best of it and worked his way forward.

3. *Not* Attaining *Position, Power, or Possessions*

In our culture, too many people believe that contentment comes from attaining material possessions or positions of power. But they aren't the keys to contentment either. If you are tempted to believe that they are, remember the words of John D. Rockefeller. When a journalist asked him how much wealth was enough, the millionaire, who was at the time one of the richest and most powerful men in the world, answered, "Just a little more."

Contentment comes from having a positive attitude. It means

- expecting the best in everything—not the worst.

- remaining upbeat—even when you get beat up.

- seeing solutions in every problem—not problems in every solution.

- believing in yourself—even when others believe you've failed.

- holding on to hope—even when others say it's hopeless.

No matter what happens to you, a positive attitude comes from within. Your circumstances and your contentment are unrelated.

POSITIVE ACTION: THE OTHER KEY TO WHAT HAPPENS IN YOU

You cannot win the internal battle against failure without the positive attitude that contentment provides. But if you think positively and do nothing, you will not be able to fail *forward*. You must add positive action to a positive attitude.

> *A problem is something that can be solved. A fact of life is something that must be accepted.*

Some people get into trouble because they focus their attention on things beyond their control. Leadership expert Fred Smith says that the key to positive action is to know the difference between a problem and a fact of life. A problem is something that can be solved. A fact of life is something that must be accepted. For example, for Greg Horn, the flood was a fact. He didn't waste his time wondering what would have happened if he had located his store elsewhere (no other grocery store in town was flooded). Not having flood insurance was a fact. So was the reality that he couldn't get into his store for days. But Greg focused on problems he could solve, such as how to raise the money to make repairs and buy new inventory, how to clean the refuse out of his building, and how to reopen for business as quickly as possible. He put his attention where it would do him some good, remained as positive as possible, and applied positive action.

It's a State of Mind

Failure is an inside job. So is success. If you want to achieve, you have to win the war in your thinking first. You can't let the failure outside you get inside you. You certainly can't control the length of your life—but you can control its width and depth. You can't control the contour of your face—but you can control its expression. You can't control the weather—but you can control the atmosphere of your mind. Why worry about things you can't control when you can keep yourself busy controlling the things that depend on you?

I read an article that highlighted the strength, courage, and resilience of the Norwegian people. Some of the toughest explorers in history have come from Norway (including Roald Amundsen, whom I wrote about in *The 21 Irrefutable Laws of Leadership*). It doesn't matter how harsh the climate or how difficult the circumstances; they always seem to persevere.

That ability has become a part of their culture. They are a nation of outdoor enthusiasts—living on the edge of the Arctic Circle. The Norwegians have a saying that I think captures their attitude: "There is no such thing as bad weather, only bad clothing."[3]

A Man Who Keeps Failure Outside

Right now you may be saying, "That's all well and good for you, John. You haven't experienced what *I* have. Even Greg Horn's story is nothing compared to mine. All he lost was money!"

If you still have a hard time believing that failure is really an inside job, then you need to hear the story of someone who maintained a winner's attitude while overcoming the most difficult circumstances.

His name is Roger Crawford, and as I write this, he's about forty years old. He makes his living as a consultant and public speaker. He has written two books and travels all across the country working with Fortune 500 companies, national and state associations, and school districts.

Those aren't bad credentials. But if they don't impress you, how about this? Before becoming a consultant, he was a varsity tennis player for Loyola Marymount University and later became a professional tennis player certified by the United States Professional Tennis Association. Still not impressed? Would you change your opinion if I told you Roger has no hands and only one foot?

No Handicap

Roger Crawford was born with a condition called *ectrodactylism*. When he emerged from his mother's womb, the doctors saw that he had a thumblike projection extending out of his right forearm, and a thumb and finger growing out of his left forearm. He had no palms. His legs and arms were shortened. And his left leg possessed a shrunken foot with only three toes. (The foot was amputated when he was five.) Various medical professionals told Roger's parents that he would never be able to walk, probably would not be able to take care of himself, and would never lead a normal life.

After recovering from the shock, Roger's parents were determined to give him the best chance possible for living a normal life. They raised him to feel loved, to be strong, and to develop independence. "You're only as handicapped as you want to be," his father used to tell him.

When he was old enough, they sent him to regular public schools. They involved him in sports. They encouraged him to do everything his heart desired. And they taught him to think positively.

"Something my parents never did was to allow me to feel sorry for myself, or to take advantage of people because of my handicap," observes Roger.[4]

If He Can Do It . . .

Roger appreciated the encouragement and training he received from his parents, but I don't think he really understood the significance or the extent of his achievements until he was in college and he interacted with someone who wanted to meet him. He had received a phone call from a man who had read about his tennis victories, and Roger agreed to meet him at a nearby restaurant. When Roger stood up to shake hands with the man, he discovered that the other guy had hands that were almost identical to his. Roger became excited because he thought he had found someone similar to him but older who could act as his mentor. But after talking with the stranger for a few minutes, he realized he was wrong. Roger explains,

> Instead, what I found was someone with a bitter, pessimistic attitude who blamed all of life's disappointments and failures on his anatomy.
>
> I soon recognized that our lives and attitudes couldn't have been different . . . He had never held a job for long, and he was sure this was because of "discrimination"—certainly not because (as he admitted) he was constantly late, frequently absent, and failed to take any responsibility for his work. His attitude was, "The world owes me," and his problem was that the world disagreed. He was even angry with me because I didn't share his despair.
>
> We kept in touch for several years, until it dawned on me that even if some miracle were suddenly to give him a perfect body, his unhappiness and lack of success wouldn't change. He would still be at the same place in his life.[5]

That man had allowed failure to seize him from the inside, while Roger had mastered the art of failing forward.

. . . You Can, Too

Chances are that the adversity in your life has been nowhere near as

> *Handicaps can only disable us if we let them. This is true not only of physical challenges, but of emotional and intellectual ones as well . . . I believe that real and lasting limitations are created in our minds, not our bodies.*
>
> —Roger Crawford

difficult as Roger Crawford's has been. And that's why his story is such an inspiration. Roger maintains, "Handicaps can only disable us if we let them. This is true not only of physical challenges, but of emotional and intellectual ones as well . . . I believe that real and lasting limitations are created in our minds, not our bodies."[6] In other words, no matter what happens, failure is an inside job.

Your Sixth Step to Failing Forward:

Don't Let the Failure from Outside Get Inside You

What in your life have you considered to be the greatest source of frustration and failure? Think about that factor, and then list all the heartaches, pains, obstacles, and problems related to it. Write them here:

Difficulties	Fact/Action Needed
1. _____	_____
2. _____	_____
3. _____	_____
4. _____	_____
5. _____	_____
6. _____	_____
7. _____	_____
8. _____	_____
9. _____	_____
10. _____	_____
11. _____	_____
12. _____	_____

Now, consider the items one at a time, and decide whether each is a fact of life (which you need to accept and then move beyond) or an item that requires positive action. For a fact of life, write "fact" next to the item, and determine to be positive despite the adversity, as Roger Crawford was. For any item needing action, in the space on the right-hand side, write down what you ought to do to create positive change in your life. Then vow to do it cheerfully.

Steps to Failing Forward:

1. Realize there is one major difference between average people and achieving people.

2. Learn a new definition of *failure*.

3. Remove the "you" from failure.

4. Take action and reduce your fear.

5. Change your response to failure by accepting responsibility.

6. Don't let the failure from outside get inside you.

7

Is the Past Holding Your Life Hostage?

*One reason God created time was so that there would
be a place to bury the failures of the past.*
—JAMES LONG

When I get a bit of time off, I like to play golf. I'm not a great golfer; I'd say I'm average. But I'm a lot better than I once was. When I first started playing golf in 1969, I was terrible. I used a baseball grip, and I tried to muscle the ball down the fairway, which caused my ball to have a big hook, often putting me in the woods and rough.

I was twenty-two years old when I started playing. Maybe I would have had an easier time if I'd started when I was five years old, as many of today's players did. Who knows? But no matter what, I'm glad I started golfing, and I can tell you who sparked my interest in the sport: Arnold Palmer.

BEFORE TIGER WOODS

Arnold Palmer is one of the great sportsmen of the twentieth century, and he really put professional golf on the map. Rick Reilly in *Sports Illustrated* wrote, "Basically, he took a game that was a little too prissy, a little too clubby, a little too saturated with Ivy League men trying not to soil their cardigans, and breathed sweet life into it." Or as Vin Scully says, "In a sport that was high society, he made it *High Noon*." That's why someone such as tour pro Rocco Mediate told Palmer during the hoopla at Palmer's last U.S. Open, "You made all this possible." Of Palmer, Tiger Woods simply stated, "He was what I wanted to be like."

Many people of my generation (I was born in 1947) became golfers because of Arnold Palmer, just as the popularity of the game today has increased because of Tiger Woods. Palmer was a consummate golf professional. Like Woods, he started playing as a small boy. And as he grew up, he performed just about every job he could on a golf course. (His father was a golf pro and course superintendent.)

Palmer has been active in professional golf for more than forty years and has won ninety-two championships, sixty-one of them on the U.S. PGA Tour. From 1960 to 1963, he was the greatest golfer in the world, winning twenty-nine PGA victories. That ability got him named *Sports Illustrated*'s Sportsman of the Year in 1960 and Athlete of the Decade according to an Associated Press poll. One writer said of Palmer that he combined "the boldness of a Brink's bandit with the fearless confidence of a man on a flying trapeze. He doesn't play a golf course, he assaults it."[1] And golf legend Bobby Jones once said, "If I ever had an eight-foot putt, and everything I owned depended on it, I'd want Arnold Palmer to take it for me."

Palmer's down-to-earth attitude, sparkling personality, rugged good looks, and incredible playing ability caused him to draw huge crowds of spectators who would follow him from hole to hole, just as Tiger Woods's fans do today. Back then they were dubbed "Arnie's Army," and it seemed they'd follow him anywhere to get a chance to see the man they called "the King" perform on the course. It was a first for golf, and it was sure fun to watch.

EVEN THE BEST STUMBLE

Any golfer can have a really bad hole—even a Hall of Famer like Arnold Palmer. The key to playing through it is to forget about your bad shots. That can be a difficult thing to do—especially when someone erects a bronze monument to your bad hole. That's what happened to Arnold Palmer.

It occurred at the 1961 Los Angeles Open at the peak of Palmer's career. On the par-5 ninth hole, his last of the day, Palmer hit a good drive and wanted to try to put the ball on the green with his second shot. He would be in position to attempt a birdie, getting one stroke closer to the leaders.

With his 3-wood, Palmer hit what he believed was a good shot. But as the ball sailed, it faded to the right, hit a pole, and bounced out of bounds onto the driving range. Palmer dropped a ball, took a penalty stroke, and tried again. This time, his ball hooked to the left and flew off the course into a road. Again he dropped a ball and took a penalty stroke. He repeated this process, hitting the ball out of bounds several times. Finally he put the ball on the green. By then, he had accumulated *ten* strokes. It took him two more strokes with his putter to hole the ball. He finished with a twelve. And because of that, he went from a few strokes behind the leaders to scoring so poorly that he was out of the tournament.

A MONUMENT TO FAILURE?

Today, nearly forty years later, if you go to the ninth hole at the Rancho Park Golf Course in Los Angeles, you will find a bronze plaque that states: "On Friday, Jan. 6, 1961, the first day of the 35th Los Angeles Open, Arnold Palmer, voted Golfer of the Year and Pro Athlete of the Year, took a 12 on this hole."

In the late 1990s I had the opportunity to meet Arnold Palmer playing golf. It was down at the Bay Hill Club in Orlando. I was playing with my brother, Larry, and there in the foursome behind us was "the King" himself. As we were winding down for the day, I teed off from the second-to-last hole, and I hooked the ball really badly. It fired over into the adjacent fairway and right at another golfer. To my horror as I yelled "fore," I realized the person about to be beaned was none other than Palmer. Fortunately he ducked.

About six months later, I received this letter in the mail:

Arnold Palmer's
BAY HILL CLUB

February 12, 1997

Dr. John Maxwell
INJOY
El Cajon, California

Dear John,

On behalf of myself and the entire staff of the Bay Hill Country Club, we would like to wish you a happy 50th birthday. As founder of the club, I extend a personal invitation to join our amateur seniors tour. It would be our privilege to have you.

John, on a personal note—When you almost decapitated me on the 17th hole last November, I made a mental note—"That swing surely is from a man about to qualify for the senior circuit." I had no idea until I saw the member birthday roster that I was so right. This unique swing now qualifies you, along with your 50th birthday, to be an elite member of our seniors club. At our lodge, just ask for the senior discount. I am sure you won't need I.D. The staff prides itself on recognizing senior ability by hair color, facial lines, and other attributes. If all else fails, just show them your swing. That'll do it!

Happy 50th birthday, John Maxwell!

Keep Swinging,

Arnold Palmer

Good golfers don't dwell on bad performances—not if they want to remain good golfers. And that has always been true of Arnold Palmer. Once when asked about his performance at the Open on hole nine, he commented, "That doggone plaque will be there long after I'm gone. But you have to put things like that behind you. That's one of the wonderful things about golf. Your next shot can be as good or bad as your last one—but you'll always get another chance."[2]

HOW THE PAST IMPACTS THE PRESENT

The same quality that makes a professional golfer effective enables any person to overcome failure and become a strong achiever: the ability to put past events behind him and move on. That quality positions a person to tackle current challenges with enthusiasm and a minimum of burdensome personal baggage.

In contrast, someone who is unable to get over previous hurts and failures is held hostage by the past. The baggage he carries around makes it very difficult for him to move forward. In fact, in more than thirty years of working with people, I have yet to meet a successful person who continually dwelled on his past difficulties.

> *In more than thirty years of working with people, I have yet to meet a successful person who continually dwelled on his past difficulties.*

A few years ago, I heard my friend Chuck Swindoll tell the story of Chippie the parakeet. He said the bird's problems began when the woman who owned him decided to clean up the seeds and loose feathers from the bottom of his cage using a vacuum. When the phone rang, the owner turned to pick it up, and—you guessed it—with a thud and a whoosh, Chippie was gone.

The owner quickly turned off the vacuum and unzipped the bag. There was Chippie. He was stunned but breathing.

Seeing that he was covered with black dust, his owner rushed Chippie to the bathtub, where she turned on the faucet full blast and held the bird under the icy water.

At that point she realized that she'd done even more damage, and she quickly cranked up her blow dryer and gave the wet, shivering little parakeet a blast. Chuck finished the story by saying, "Chippie doesn't sing much anymore . . ."

People who are unable to overcome the past are a little like Chippie. They allow their negative experiences to color the way they live their lives today.

It may sound as if I'm making light of what may have happened to you in the past. I'm not. I know that people suffer genuine tragedies in this imperfect world. They lose children, spouses, parents, and friends—sometimes under horrible circumstances. (My dad lost his mother before he was eight years old.) People contract cancer, multiple sclerosis, AIDS, and other debilitating diseases. They suffer unspeakable abuses at the hands of others. All of these things are true. But tragedies don't have to stop a person from possessing a positive outlook, being productive, and living life to the fullest. One man is born with severe disabilities and decides the world owes him, while another (such as Roger Crawford) goes on to become a tennis pro. One person who contracts AIDS bitterly gives up on life, while another (such as basketball's Magic Johnson) builds his business and enjoys his family life. One woman experiences rape and withdraws into herself, while another (such as Kelly McGillis) overcomes the experience and becomes a successful actress in Hollywood. No matter how dark a person's past is, it need not color his present permanently.

SIGNS OF PAST BREAKDOWN

In my experience, the problems of people's pasts impact them in one of two ways: They experience either a breakdown or a breakthrough. The following five characteristics are signs that people haven't gotten over past difficulties:

1. Comparison

If you hear people continually talk about how much harder they've had it than anyone else, chances are, they are allowing themselves to be held

> *The problems of people's pasts impact them in one of two ways: They experience either a breakdown or a breakthrough.*

hostage by their past. Their motto is similar to something Quentin Crisp once said: "Never keep up with the Joneses. Drag them down to your level. It's cheaper."

2. Rationalization

Another characteristic of people trapped by their pasts is rationalization: believing that there are good reasons not to get over past difficulties. Rationalization creates a fog that hinders people from finding solutions to their problems. Excuses, no matter how strong, never lead to achievement.

3. Isolation

As I've mentioned, some people withdraw due to their past hurts. For many, it's like a natural reflex that kicks in for self-protection. When naturally outgoing people isolate themselves because of the past, they become especially miserable.

Author C. S. Lewis asserted, "We are born helpless. As soon as we are fully conscious we discover loneliness. We need others physically, emotionally, intellectually; we need them if we are to know anything, even ourselves."

4. Regret

A significant hindrance to living life in the present is regret. It saps people's energy and leaves little enabling them to do anything positive.

My friend Dwight Bain E-mailed me something called "The City of Regret" that tells the whole story:

I had not really planned to take a trip this year, yet I found myself packing anyway. And off I went, dreading it. I was on another guilt trip.

I booked my reservation on *Wish I Had* airlines. I didn't check my bags—everyone carries their baggage on this airline—and had to drag it for what seemed like miles in the Regret City airport. And I could see that people from all over the world were there with me, limping along under the weight of bags they had packed themselves.

I caught a cab to Last Resort Hotel, the driver taking the whole trip backward, looking over his shoulder. And there I found the ballroom where my event would be held: the Annual Pity Party. As I checked in, I saw that all my old colleagues were on the guest list:

The Done family—Woulda, Coulda, and Shoulda
Both of the Opportunities—Missed and Lost
All the Yesterdays—there were too many to count, but all would have sad stories to share
Shattered Dreams and Broken Promises would be there, too, along with their friends Don't Blame Me and Couldn't Help It.

And of course, hours and hours of entertainment would be provided by that renowned storyteller *It's Their Fault.*

As I prepared to settle in for a really long night, I realized that one person had the power to send all those people home and break up the party: me. All I had to do was return to the present and welcome the new day!

If you have found yourself getting on a flight to the City of Regret, recognize that it's a trip you book yourself, and you can cancel it at any time—without penalty or fee. But you're the only one who can.

5. Bitterness

People who don't get beyond the problems or the pain of the past eventually become bitter. It is the inevitable consequence of not processing old injuries and tragedies.

Wes Roberts, president of Life Enrichment, advises, "People do not have to remain victims of their pasts." But when they do, they become prisoners of their own emotions. "Often as adults, those prisons are addictions—workaholism, alcoholism, sexual addictions, eating addictions. We place ourselves in prison." In other words, we allow the past to hold us hostage.

No matter what you've experienced, remember this: There are people who've had it better than you and done worse. And there are people who've had it worse than you and done better. The circumstances really have nothing to do with getting over your personal history. Past hurts can make you bitter or better—the choice is yours.

BREAKTHROUGH: THE ALTERNATIVE TO BREAKDOWN

Every major difficulty you face in life is a fork in the road. You choose which track you will head down, toward breakdown or breakthrough.

Dick Biggs, a consultant who helps Fortune 500 companies improve profits and increase productivity, writes that all of us have unfair experiences; as a result, some people merely exist and adopt a "cease and desist" mentality. He continues,

> *Every major difficulty you face in life is a fork in the road. You choose which track you will head down, toward breakdown or breakthrough.*

One of the best teachers of persistence is your life's critical turning points. Expect to experience 3–9 turning points or "significant changes" in your life. These transitions can be happy experiences . . . or unhappy times such as job losses, divorce, financial setbacks, health problems and the death of loved ones. Turning points can provide perspective, which is the ability to view major changes within the larger framework of your lifetime and let the healing power of time prevail. By learning from your turning points, you can grow at a deeper level within your career and life.[3]

If you've been badly hurt, then start by acknowledging the pain and grieving any loss you may have experienced. Then forgive the people involved—including yourself, if needed. Doing that will help you move on. (If you cannot accomplish that on your own, enlist the help of a professional.)

I understand that it may be very difficult to go through this process, but you can do it. Just think, *today* may be your day to turn the hurts of your past into a breakthrough for the future. Don't allow anything from your personal history to keep holding you hostage.

A DREAM BECKONS TO THE EAST

One person who always traveled light (without too much personal baggage) was Sister Frances Cabrini. On the March day in 1889 when the thirty-eight-year-old nun got off the boat at Ellis Island, she was thinking about the task ahead of her: helping establish an orphanage, school, and convent in New York City. She wasn't preoccupied with any of the problems from her past, though she had experienced plenty.

Francesca Lodi-Cabrini was born two months premature in the Lombardy town of Sant'Angelo, Italy, where she remained the sickliest child in her village as she grew up. At age six, she decided that she wanted to become a missionary to China. However, people mocked her dream.

"A missionary order would never accept a girl who is ill most of the time," her sister Rosa scoffed.

At age twelve, she took a vow of chastity, and when she reached the required minimum age of eighteen, she applied to join the Daughters of the Sacred Heart Convent. But she was indeed rejected because she was too sickly.

Rejection was not going to make Cabrini give up her dream of ministering in Asia. She began doing what she could in her own village to build her strength and prove her worth. She taught neighborhood children. She cared for an older villager. And when a smallpox epidemic hit, she nursed family and friends through it until she became sick. After she recovered, she reapplied to the convent. She was turned down again.

A STEP FORWARD

After six years, Cabrini finally gained acceptance into the order. She thought that milestone would put her one step closer to achieving her dream of serving in China. But she was to experience many additional setbacks. Both her parents died within a year. Then she was assigned to teach at a local school rather than one overseas. When she applied to other organizations devoted to working in Asia, she was rejected. Soon she was assigned to oversee a small orphanage in Codogno, a town not more than fifty miles from her home. She spent six frustrating years there before the orphanage was closed down.

When she still dreamed of traveling to Asia, a superior told her that if she wanted to be part of a missionary order, she should start one herself. So that's what she did. With the assistance of a half-dozen girls from the orphanage, she founded the Missionary Sisters of the Sacred Heart in 1880. During the next eight years, she built the order, establishing foundations in Milan, Rome, and other Italian cities.

She tried to earn a place in Asia, but Pope Leo XIII put an end to Cabrini's dream of ministering in China. He told her, "Not to the east, but to the west. You will find a vast field of labor in the United States." She was to help run an orphanage, school, and convent in New York City.

A TRIP WEST

That is how Sister Frances Cabrini came to be at Ellis Island in March 1889. Her lifelong dream of serving in Asia lay in ruins behind her in Italy, the only home she'd ever known. But she didn't look back. She was not someone to allow the past to hold her hostage.

Over the next twenty-eight years, she dedicated herself to the task of ministering to people in the Americas. And she overcame plenty of obstacles to do it. When she arrived in New York, she was told that the plans for the orphanage, school, and convent had fallen through, and that she should return to Italy. Instead, she solved the problems they were having and established the facilities as planned.

It didn't matter what difficulties she faced, she continually overcame them. By the time she died in 1917 at age sixty-seven, she had founded more than seventy hospitals, schools, and orphanages in the United States, Spain, France, England, and South America.

Cabrini's impact was incredible. She was the Mother Teresa of her day—possessing similar compassion, grit, tenacity, and leadership. But she never would have made a difference if she had allowed her past to hold her hostage. Instead of lamenting the loss of her dream and the hurts of her youth, she moved on and did what she could where God put her. My hope is that you can do the same.

Your Seventh Step to Failing Forward:

Say Good-bye to Yesterday

To move forward today, you must learn to say good-bye to yesterday's hurts, tragedies, and baggage. You can't build a monument to past problems and fail forward.

Take time right now to list the negative events from your past that may be holding you hostage:

For each item you listed, go through the following process.

1. Acknowledge the pain.

2. Grieve the loss.

3. Forgive the person.

4. Forgive yourself.

5. Determine to release the event and move on.

If you are having a hard time because you're holding grudges, talk to God about the issue and ask Him to help you through the process. No matter how difficult this becomes, persevere through it. You will not be able to be your best today until you say good-bye to yesterday.

Steps to Failing Forward:

1. Realize there is one major difference between average people and achieving people.

2. Learn a new definition of *failure*.

3. Remove the "you" from failure.

4. Take action and reduce your fear.

5. Change your response to failure by accepting responsibility.

6. Don't let the failure from outside get inside you.

7. Say good-bye to yesterday.

8

Who Is This Person Making
These Mistakes?

Failure is the greatest opportunity I have to know who I really am.
—JOHN KILLINGER

Sometimes great achievement can come *only* as the result of a period of failure that helps you understand who you really are. That was the case for John James Audubon, the man for whom the National Audubon Society was named. His life was one of extremes—problems and progress, struggle and success, failure and fanfare. Here is his story.

AUDUBON'S BEGINNINGS

The son of a French sea captain, Audubon was born in Haiti in 1785, but spent his formative years in France. He was educated as a gentleman, but was at best an indifferent student. Because of his lack of discipline, he was sent to military school at age fourteen, but he didn't flourish in that environment either. His real passion was hunting and drawing birds.

At age eighteen, Audubon was sent to America. His father felt that opportunity lay in the New World. Audubon landed in Pennsylvania and moved into a house his father owned there. In his new surroundings he honed his skills as a woodsman. He continued hunting and drawing wildlife, and it wasn't long before he met and developed a relationship with a neighboring family named the Bakewells. They had a significant impact on his life. First, he fell in love with one of the family's daughters, Lucy. Second, in 1807, he started working in the counting house of Benjamin Bakewell's import company. That was the start of what would become an abysmal career in business.

A CAREER IN TRADE

Audubon's first venture, which dealt in indigo dye, was indicative of his performance: It lost him a small fortune. He worked at the import business for a while, but after meeting no success, Audubon decided to try his hand at retail trade. Through his father's connections, he hooked up with Ferdinand Rozier, a young French businessman, and the two men headed west to Louisville, Kentucky, on the banks of the Ohio River.

They set up for business, but met with minimal success. Rozier possessed tenacity for trade while Audubon displayed the qualities that marked his entire life: hunting skill, undisciplined curiosity, unfailing energy, and artistic power. While Rozier manned the counter in the shop, Audubon roamed the countryside hunting and bringing back birds to be drawn or served at the table.

During that time, Audubon's favorite contributions to the business were his trips to Philadelphia and New York to purchase goods for the store because he had a chance to see the countryside. On one of those trips, he returned to Pennsylvania and married Lucy Bakewell and took her back to Louisville with him.

The partners worked together for a while, but it wasn't long before the business was in trouble financially. To raise the needed money, Audubon sold Lucy's share of her family's estate and paid off their creditors.

MAKING CHANGES

The partners then decided that a new location would help them, and they went downstream to Henderson, Kentucky. They lasted six months there and then made another change in location, this time to the banks of the Mississippi River. After much difficulty, they set up shop in Ste. Genevieve, Missouri, a settlement of French Canadians.

As before, Audubon wasn't content with the business of trade and spent most of his time hunting birds, then drawing and painting them. After a short time, he sold his share in the shop, and the two partners went their separate ways. Rozier kept the business and became highly successful. Audubon went in search of another opportunity. Audubon's biographer, John Chancellor, asserted, "Audubon believed that he should persevere in commerce and that shooting, mounting and drawing birds should remain an absorbing hobby."

MORE FAILURES

Over the next ten years, Audubon embarked on a series of unsuccessful ventures. In 1811, he decided to return to the import business. He and his brother-in-law, Thomas Woodhouse Bakewell, established a commission house in New Orleans importing goods from England. Unfortunately they did that on the eve of the War of 1812. Of course, their business failed.

Audubon and his brother-in-law went back to work in trading goods—again in Henderson, Kentucky. They saw some success there, but then they made another poor business decision. They chose to open a steam sawmill and gristmill in an area that could not support such a large operation. By 1819, they had gone bankrupt.

All through the years, two things remained constant in Audubon's life: hunting and art. Now he had to rely on both to survive. His gun put food on the table for his small family (he and Lucy had two young boys by then), and he drew portraits on commission to bring in money. By default rather than design, his hobby became his means of support.

FINALLY THE RIGHT KIND OF CHANGE

In 1820, Audubon had what he called his "Great Idea." He decided to create a comprehensive and complete printed collection of all American birds based on his paintings. They would be life-size and shown in their natural surroundings. For the next few years, he traveled and added more painted birds to his portfolio while Lucy worked as a tutor and governess in Louisiana.

By 1826, he had enough material. Audubon sailed to Liverpool, England, and immediately met with great success. He wrote back to his wife, Lucy, "I am well received everywhere, my works praised and admired, and my poor heart is at the last relieved from the great anxiety that has for so many years agitated it, for I now know that I have not worked in vain."

Audubon became associated with engraver Robert Havell, and together they began printing the remarkable *Birds of America*, a series of one hundred color plates in a large 29-by-39-inch format. Audubon wrote of the effort, "Who would believe that a lonely individual, who landed in England without a friend in the whole country, and with only sufficient pecuniary means to travel through it as a visitor, could have accomplished such a task as this publication?"

The publication of his book finally gave him financial security—and it made him famous all over Europe and the United States. Nothing else like it had ever been created, nor has any other book of prints since been so revered. In all, they printed about two hundred copies of that first edition. Today it's considered a masterpiece. An original *Birds of America*, which sold for $1,000 in the 1820s, is now worth about $5 million!

THE PROBLEM WAS HIM

John James Audubon was unsuccessful for most of his life. It took him until he was thirty-five years old to figure out what his problem was: himself. He was a terrible businessman, and he didn't belong in trade. It didn't matter how many times he changed locations, partners, or business types. Not until he understood and changed himself did he have a chance at success. For years this saying could have applied to him: If you could kick the person responsible for most of your troubles, you wouldn't be able to sit down for weeks.

Evangelist D. L. Moody was once asked which people gave him the most trouble. His response was, "I've had more trouble with Dwight L.

Moody than any other man alive." Television host Jack Paar echoed that same thought: "Looking back, my life seems like one long obstacle race, with me as its chief obstacle." If you are continually experiencing trouble or facing obstacles, then you should check to make sure that *you* are not the problem.

WHY WON'T PEOPLE CHANGE?

People don't like to admit that they need to change. And if they are willing to alter things about themselves, they usually focus on cosmetic changes. Perhaps that's why Emerson said, "People are always getting ready to live but never living." Yet anyone who wants to live in a better world needs to be willing to change himself. Psychiatrist Rudolf Dreikurs, director of the Alfred Adler Institute of Chicago, observed, "We can change our whole life and the attitude of people around us simply by changing ourselves."

> *We can change our whole life and the attitude of people around us simply by changing ourselves.*
>
> —RUDOLF DREIKURS

Why are people so hesitant to change? I believe that some, like Audubon, believe they are supposed to pursue a particular course of action for some reason—even though it doesn't suit their gifts and talents. And when they are not working in areas of strength, they do poorly. Others are not self-aware and don't even know what their strengths are. As Ben Franklin noted, "There are three things extremely hard: steel, a diamond, and to know one's self." Still others hinder themselves.

I read an article about a nineteenth-century French chess champion named Alexandre Deschapelles. He was a great player who quickly became a champion in his region. But when competition got tough, he decided that he would play an opponent only if the person would remove one of Deschapelles's pawns and then make the first move. That way, he would not look bad no matter what happened. If he lost, he could say

91

that he had been at a disadvantage. If he won, he would seem that much more talented. Today, psychologists call that mind-set the Deschapelles Coup.

THERE'S NOTHING WRONG WITH CHANGING YOUR MIND

Psychologist Sheldon Kopp says, "All of the significant battles are waged within the self." That's true. People wage the greatest battles against their own flaws and failures.

For years, John James Audubon must have regarded his desire to grab his gun and sketch pad and disappear into the woods as a fatal flaw because he thought he should be running a business. But when he realized that his gun and notepad were the tools of his business, everything became clearer in his mind.

> *All of the significant battles are waged within the self.*
> —SHELDON KOPP

Successful television producer and film director Garry Marshall, a self-described late bloomer, has experienced more than his share of failures. You're probably familiar with some of his successes: the movie *Pretty Woman* and television's *The Odd Couple, Laverne and Shirley,* and *Happy Days.* But chances are, you don't remember some of his other efforts, such as *Blansky's Beauties* and *Me and the Chimp.* They were bombs.

"Most people try to beat down their flaws or deny them altogether," notes Marshall. "I've always found it best to say, 'Here are my flaws. Now I have to find something I'm good at.' Don't use your flaws as an excuse to quit. Move forward or sideways."[1]

MOVING FORWARD OR SIDEWAYS

The character Jean Valjean in Victor Hugo's *Les Misérables* declared, "It is nothing to die. It is an awful thing never to have lived." That's what it's like for people who deny their internal flaws, bury them, and then try to pretend that they don't exist. To have an opportunity to reach your potential, you must know who you are and face your flaws. Allow me to help you do that. Go through the following process:

1. See Yourself Clearly

Bishop Fulton Sheen offered this insight, "Most of us do not like to look inside ourselves for the same reason we don't like to open a letter that has bad news." Many people see all the bad and deny the good, or they see all the good and deny the bad. To reach your potential, you must see both.

2. Admit Your Flaws Honestly

In Chapter 5 I stated that you must take responsibility for *your actions* to fail forward. But you must also take responsibility for who *you are as a person*. That means owning up to what you cannot do (based on skill), should not do (based on talent), and ought not do (based on character). That's not always easy to do.

3. Discover Your Strengths Joyfully

Working on your strengths is the next step in the process. No one ever achieved his dreams working outside his areas of gifting. To excel, do what you do well.

4. Build on Those Strengths Passionately

Like Audubon, you will improve only if you enthusiastically develop your God-given abilities. You can reach your potential tomorrow if you dedicate yourself to growth today. Remember, to change your world, you must first change yourself.

WHO IS THIS PERSON?

One of the greatest stories of change that I know personally involves someone very close to me in my organization, The INJOY Group. As I worked on this book and was thinking about whose story I should tell in this chapter, my assistant, Linda Eggers, suggested that maybe her story would help you understand the impact that changing yourself can make on your life.

If you've ever heard me speak in person, then you've probably heard me talk about Linda. I believe that Linda is the finest executive assistant in the country. But I haven't always felt that way about her. A few years ago we experienced a rocky time in our history, and the fact that we work together now is a strong testament to her willingness and ability to take a hard look at her-

> *To excel, do what you do well.*

self, make some changes in her life, and become the kind of person she desired to be.

Linda began working for me in the mid-1980s when I was leading Skyline Church in San Diego as its senior pastor. She had a job in the financial office with Steve Babby, our CFO. It was also about that time that I formed The INJOY Group with the help of my good friend Dick Peterson. Back then we functioned on a shoestring, and our "staff" consisted of a handful of volunteers, including Linda and her husband, Patrick.

HELPING BUILD THE TEAM

After Linda had been working with me for a while, I invited her to attend a new conference I was teaching in southern California. During the course of that conference, Linda realized that she felt called to work with me at INJOY, helping me to equip pastors to become better leaders. She approached me after the conference and shared her thoughts with me. Later when INJOY was big enough, we brought her on staff.

Linda immediately became an impact player for us under the leadership of Dick Peterson, now the COO of The INJOY Group and president of INJOY Conferences and Resources. Linda did whatever was asked of her, and that was just about everything. She managed the office, hired staff, performed accounting tasks, and even assisted with product development. As we grew, she took on greater and greater responsibility. By the early 1990s, she was Dick's right hand.

MAKING THESE MISTAKES

Then suddenly one day, Linda quit. She gave two weeks' notice, and she was gone. She didn't give any explanation; she simply bailed on us. Dick and I were shocked.

A few weeks later I found out that Linda had gone to work for an accountant friend of mine as his secretary. I was amazed because she had always been passionate about the kind of work we did. I couldn't see her being happy merely typing letters and doing simple data entry.

Then something even more surprising happened. I heard that Linda was becoming very negative about me and INJOY. She wasn't being malicious, but her comments were inappropriate. And that saddened me because I always liked her.

Meanwhile, life went on. Dick hired someone to replace Linda, and the company continued its growth. About eight months later, I got a phone call telling me Linda wanted to see me. On the day that she came to my office, she was shaking. And as she talked, she started to cry. She apologized for all the negative things she had been saying. Then she told me why she quit and what led to her feelings of bitterness.

"I was working so hard and so many hours," Linda said, "that it was killing me. I thought nobody cared. I realize now that I should have gone to Dick or come to you and told you how I was feeling. But I was in performance mode, and I was too proud to cry 'uncle.' Then I started a pity-me party. John, I am very sorry."

Linda went on to say that it took her only a month at her new job to realize she had made a big mistake; she should have stayed at INJOY.

"What are you going to do now?" I asked.

"I don't know. I'm not going to stay where I am because I've handled that poorly too. I guess I'm going to look for a job."

"Would you ever think about coming back to INJOY?" I asked.

"Do you think you could trust me again?" she replied.

"I don't know . . . ," I said.

Later that day, Dick told me that Linda had met and apologized to him too. She also apologized to her current employer.

Dick and I talked about it, and he offered to hire her back. But it would be in a different capacity. The only thing available at the time was a position taking incoming calls and answering correspondence. It must have been difficult for Linda, who had once been Dick's second in command, but she accepted. For three years, Linda worked hard and did everything asked of her with excellence and a positive attitude, and over time, she began to assist Dick more and more.

HELPING MAKE A DIFFERENCE

When I left the pastorate at Skyline in 1995 to devote myself full-time to The INJOY Group, I needed to hire a new assistant. And one of the people I considered was Linda. I knew she was highly competent; the only issue I needed to settle was whether I could trust her unconditionally. An executive assistant who works with me has to be capable of running my life, dealing with sensitive and personal information about me and my family, and representing me well with everyone.

It didn't take me long to settle the issue. I knew I wanted Linda to be my assistant. Since that day, I've never looked back or doubted her. In fact, if she hadn't courageously suggested I tell her story, it never would have occurred to me to share it.

After Linda started working with me again, she told me something interesting. "From the early days when I worked at Skyline back in '86," she said, "I always believed that someday I would be your assistant. And to think that I almost blew it! The turning point for me was the day I looked at myself in the mirror and realized that I needed to make some changes in my life—starting with my attitude. If I hadn't, I never would have gotten the opportunity to do the work that I believe God put me here to do."

Today, Linda is awesome. I marvel at what she is capable of doing. And every time I make a positive impact on anyone with a conference or book, she is a part of it. I wouldn't trade her for anyone else in the world.

As you read this, if you are not happy with your current job, family situation, or life, look first at what you can change in yourself before trying to alter your circumstances. And recognize this:

Not *realizing* what you want is a problem of *knowledge*.
Not *pursuing* what you want is a problem of *motivation*.
Not *achieving* what you want is a problem of *persistence*.

If you know who you are, make the changes you must in order to learn and grow, and then give everything you've got to your dreams, you can achieve anything your heart desires.

Your Eighth Step to Failing Forward:

Change Yourself, and Your World Changes

Sam Peeples Jr. says, "The circumstances of life, the events of life, and the people around me in life do not *make* me the way I am, but *reveal* the way I am." Take some time to discover who you are by examining your weaknesses and strengths.

First, list evident weaknesses or flaws:

MY WEAKNESSES

Personal Observations:

Observations from Those Closest to Me:

Observations from Other People:

Weaknesses require change. If something you listed falls into the category of attitude or character, you need to do an about-face, as Linda Eggers did. (It may require an apology, restitution, or changes in lifestyle.) If a weakness you listed has to do with an absence of talent or skill, then you may need to make adjustments in your priorities, goals, or career.

Now, think about your strengths. List the gifts, talents, opportunities, and resources you possess:

MY STRENGTHS

Giftedness:

Skills:

Opportunities:

Resources:

Develop a plan that will allow you to build on the strengths and maximize your potential. Remember, you cannot change without unless you change within. Change yourself, and your whole world changes.

Steps to Failing Forward:

1. Realize there is one major difference between average people and achieving people.

2. Learn a new definition of *failure.*

3. Remove the "you" from failure.

4. Take action and reduce your fear.

5. Change your response to failure by accepting responsibility.

6. Don't let the failure from outside get inside you.

7. Say good-bye to yesterday.

8. Change yourself, and your world changes.

9

Get Over Yourself—Everyone Else Has

*Don't get stuck inside your own ego,
because it will become a prison in no time flat.*
—BARBARA WARD

People who desire to fail forward must turn their attention away from themselves and toward helping others. You could call that process *getting over yourself*. A few years ago, I saw a wonderful movie called *Mr. Holland's Opus* that beautifully illustrated the whole process.

IT STARTED AS A THANK-YOU

The movie was written by screenwriter Patrick Sheane Duncan, who came up with the idea one day while stuck in a traffic jam. He heard a news report on the radio about the cutback in school programs and the number of teachers in the state of California.

"Suddenly I realized how important my own teachers had been in my life," says Duncan, "and that the most important thing we can do as adults is educate our children."

Duncan remembered the one special teacher who made a difference in his life. "She was reputed to be the meanest and toughest teacher at my junior high," he recalls. "But she was the one who bought me my books and gave me her own son's clothing after he'd grown out of them. *Mr. Holland's Opus* is a tribute to her and everyone else in her grand profession."

ONE MAN'S JOURNEY

The movie is the story of Glenn Holland (played by Richard Dreyfuss), a young musician who desires to make it to the big time as a composer. But when money gets tight, and he needs to take care of his family, he reluctantly seeks employment as a teacher. That job, which he takes only on a temporary basis, becomes his life. Through the course of the movie, he discovers that he wants to share his love for music with his students, and in the process, he discovers himself.

The pivotal point of the movie comes when Mr. Holland's teaching position is eliminated because of cutbacks, and he suddenly realizes he has reached middle age. In that moment, he knows that he has forever missed his chance to pull up roots, go to New York, and take his symphony with him, which he has been writing in his spare moments for the last twenty years. Despondent and feeling rejected, he believes he has wasted his life.

He is depressed and on the verge of bitterness, as he leaves his classroom. He ambles dejectedly down the hall, preparing to walk out of the school for the last time. That's when he hears something in the auditorium. When he checks to see what it is, he discovers dozens and dozens of students whose lives he changed during all his years of teaching. That group even includes the governor of the state, whose life took a major turn for the better under his mentoring.

AN ORDINARY MAN DOING SOMETHING EXTRAORDINARY

The director of the movie, Stephen Herek, was attracted to *Mr. Holland's Opus* because the screenplay touched him. "It made me cry," he admitted. "Very rarely do I read something where I actually end up with tears flowing freely. But that's how I felt at the end of [the script]. The story makes a hero out of an Everyman who happens to be a teacher, which I think is an important thing to do. . . . It's also a story about how one human being can affect a lot of other people and touch their lives in a very special way."

Many people believe that touching the lives of others can be done only by some elite group of specially gifted people. But that's not the case. Any ordinary person—just like Glenn Holland in the movie—can make a positive impact on the lives of others.

Some unsuccessful people tell themselves that as soon as they achieve considerable success or discover some unseen talent, they will turn their attention to making a difference in the lives of others. But I have news for them. Many people who struggle with chronic failure do so *because* they think of no one but themselves. They worry about what other people think of them. They scramble to make sure no one gets the better of them. They continually focus on protecting their turf.

> *Many people who struggle with chronic failure do so* because *they think of no one but themselves.*

Years ago I read an article about New York Yankees manager Billy Martin that described him as a person who acted that way. The author said that in his later years, the former ballplayer spent much of his energy second-guessing supposed enemies and foiling imaginary plots against him. I don't know to what extent that is true, but I do know this: Martin was hired and fired from his position as Yankees manager *five* times.

My dad loves to tell jokes, and the cornier they are, the better he likes them. I recall going to an NFL ball game with him in San Diego, and as the Chargers huddled up, he leaned over to me and said, "John, did you hear about the guy who quit going to football games? Every time the team huddled up, he thought they were talking about him!"

If you continually focus all your energy and attention on yourself, I have a message for you: *Get over yourself—everyone else has.*

If you have a history of repeated failure *and* you dedicate most of your time and energy to looking out for number one, you may need to learn a new way of thinking—where others come first. If you suspect that a selfish streak is preventing you from achieving your goals and dreams, you may need to change and improve your approach to success.

STOP FOCUSING ON YOURSELF

First, you need to think about others rather than yourself. A major cause of negative thinking and poor mental health is self-absorption. Selfishness ultimately hurts not only the people around a self-focused person, but also the selfish person himself. It inclines the person toward failure because it keeps him in a negative mental rut.

That is the reason that Dr. Karl Menninger responded the way he did when someone asked, "What would you advise a person to do if he felt a nervous breakdown coming on?" Most people expected him to reply, "Consult a psychiatrist," since that was his profession. To their astonishment, Menninger replied, "Lock up your house, go across the railway tracks, find someone in need, and do something to help that person."[1]

> *Generous people are rarely mentally ill people.*
> —KARL MENNINGER

My friend Kevin Myers points out that "most people are too insecure to give anything away." I believe that's true. Most people who focus all their attention on themselves feel that they're missing something in their lives, so they're trying to get it back. For example, here are some needs and the common side effects that occur when they're missing:

Inner Need	If Missing, I Feel . . .
Belonging	Insecure
Worth	Inferior
Competence	Inadequate
Purpose	Insignificant

Developing a giving spirit, as Menninger implied, helps a person to overcome some feelings of deficiency in a positive and healthy way. That's why Menninger believed that "generous people are rarely mentally ill people." A person is less likely to focus on himself if he is trying to help someone else.

STOP TAKING YOURSELF TOO SERIOUSLY

In my seminars, I work with a lot of leaders. And I've found that many of them take themselves much too seriously. Of course, they're not alone. I meet people in every walk of life who have too much doom and gloom in their attitudes. They need to lighten up. No matter how serious your work is, that's no reason to take *yourself* seriously.

A few weeks ago, I was in Australia teaching leadership to a group of several thousand businesspeople. And I was talking to them about how most of us think that we are more important than we really are. I told everyone that on the day I die, one of my good pastor friends will give me a wonderful eulogy and tell funny stories about me, but twenty minutes later the most important thing he'll have on his mind will be trying to find the potato salad at my reception. You need to have a sense of humor about these things—especially if you work with people. Comedian Victor Borge summed it up: "Laughter is the shortest distance between two people."

If any person had a reason to take his job and himself seriously, it is the president of the United States. Yet it's possible for even people holding that position to maintain their sense of humor and keep their egos in check. For example, when Calvin Coolidge was asked if he would attend the Sesquicentennial Exposition in Philadelphia, the president answered, "Yes."

"Why are you going, Mr. President?" a reporter asked.

"As an exhibit," answered Coolidge.

More recently, when George Bush was told that a company would be selling a set of presidential trading cards for kids, his response was, "I don't dare ask how many hundreds of George Bush cards you have to trade to get one Michael Jordan."

If you tend to take yourself too seriously, give yourself and everyone else around you a break. Recognize that laughter breeds resilience.

START PUTTING THE TEAM FIRST

If you follow sports these days, you've heard a lot of talk about the selfishness of professional athletes. The recent criticism has been especially harsh toward pro basketball players because the feeling is that too many players possess a me-first mentality. Critics often point to the difference in performance between the men's and the women's basketball teams in the 1996 Olympics. The amount of talent on the men's team far outweighed that of their opponents, yet the players sometimes found it difficult to play together as a team. Meanwhile, the women virtually defined teamwork with their performance.

When competition is fierce, selfishness makes it almost impossible for a team to win. It ultimately produces failure. If talent alone won championships, then the Los Angeles Lakers of the late 1990s would have earned one.

Fortunately all of the stories out of the NBA aren't about selfishness and failure. The 1999 NBA champions—the San Antonio Spurs—won their victory because the man who had been their best player for a decade knew the importance of getting over himself.

Standing at seven feet one inch, David Robinson is the center for the Spurs. In his ten years in the NBA, Robinson has earned just about every type of award there is for a professional basketball player: Rookie of the Year (1990), Rebounding Champion (1991), Defensive Player of the Year (1992), #1 Shot Blocker (1992), #1 Scorer (1994), and Most Valuable Player (1995). He has also been named to the NBA All-Star team eight times. His consistently excellent play has put him in the upper echelon statistically in several all-time NBA categories, including points scored per game. He has been named one of the fifty greatest players in NBA history.

Despite all of Robinson's personal achievements, he had never won an NBA championship—until the 1999 season. How did he do it? By giving up the ball offensively and allowing another player, Tim Duncan, to be the hero.

During the 1999 play-offs, teammate Avery Johnson commented, "What we have in David Robinson is the ultimate team player, the ultimate winner. He threw his ego out and became a totally different player for the good of the team. He could still average 25 points. But would we be where we are? No."

In 1999, Robinson put up the lowest averages of his career. His viewpoint was this: "I looked at our team and realized we needed me to be more defensive and rebounding-minded. To be a complete team, both of us didn't need to score. Some nights I might, but it's Tim's team. And I'm fine with that."

The result of Robinson's unselfish ability to put the team ahead of himself was success for *everyone* on the team. If you want to win and overcome failure, you've got to get over yourself.

START ADDING VALUE TO OTHERS CONTINUALLY

When people think about you, do they say to themselves, "My life is better because of that person," or "My life is worse"? Their response probably answers the question of whether you are adding value to them. Since we moved to Atlanta a few years ago, we've made some new friends named Howard and Doris Bowen. Not long ago, my wife, Margaret, and I attended a birthday party for Doris. A lot of people attended that party because of the positive impact she's had on their lives. As we sat listening, person after person stood up to talk about the difference she had made in his or her life.

Doris is an extra-mile person. After I had a heart attack in December 1998, there came a time when I had to go into the hospital all day for tests. Doris dropped everything to spend that nerve-racking day with Margaret, even though we'd only just met her. Doris is always doing that kind of thing for others. She's a wonderful friend.

After all of the people at the party told Doris how much she meant to them, she stood up and said, "All my life I've wanted people to feel like they were better for knowing me. Thank you for making me feel like I've made a difference."

To succeed personally, you must try to help others. That's why my friend Zig Ziglar says, "You can get everything in life you want if you help enough other people get what they want." How do you do that? How can you turn your focus from yourself and start adding value to others? You can do it by . . .

1. Putting Others First in Your Thinking

When you meet people, is your first thought about what they'll think of you or how you can make them feel more comfortable? At work, do you try to make your coworkers or employees look good, or are you more concerned about making sure that you receive your share of the credit? When you interact with family members, whose best interests do you have in mind?

> *When you know people's values, you can add value to them.*

Your answers show where your heart is. To add value to others, you need to start putting others ahead of yourself in your mind and heart. If you can do it there, you will be able to put them first in your actions.

2. Finding Out What Others Need

How can anyone add value to others if he doesn't know *what* they care about? Listen to people. Ask them what matters to them. And observe them. If you can discover how people spend their time and money, you'll know what they value. And when you know people's values, you can add value to them.

3. Meeting That Need with Excellence and Generosity

The final step requires concrete action. Once you know what matters to people, do your best to meet their needs with excellence and generosity. Offer your best with no thought toward what you might receive in return.

President Calvin Coolidge believed that "no enterprise can exist for itself alone. It ministers to some great need, it performs some great service, not for itself, but for others; or failing therein it ceases to be profitable and ceases to exist."

BEHIND EVERY GREAT MAN

When I think of some of the notable figures in history who were able to minister to people's needs and perform great service, one of the first who comes to mind is John Wesley, the eighteenth-century Briton who founded the Methodist movement. He was a leader who served God unselfishly his entire life. But I consider someone else in his family to have been more selfless than he was and, in fact, to have made his achievements possible through her service.

> *No enterprise can exist for itself alone. It ministers to some great need, it performs some great service, not for itself, but for others; or failing therein it ceases to be profitable and ceases to exist.*
>
> —CALVIN COOLIDGE

That person was John's mother, Susanna Wesley. Born the twenty-fourth child of a well-to-do family in London in 1669, the highly intelligent Susanna was the "pet" of her father, clergyman Samuel Annesley. Though daughters were not usually given formal education in England at that time, Susanna received excellent instruction from her father and was also allowed to be in his study when the many famous men of the time congregated there to debate current issues and philosophy. As a result, she was well informed, and her intellect was razor sharp.

At age nineteen, she married Samuel Wesley, a young clergyman who came to be regarded as one of the finest scholars of his day. They set up household and began their life together. Before long, Susanna bore their first child, and then many more followed. Unfortunately their hopes were greater than their prospects, and they spent their nearly fifty years of marriage barely scraping by financially.

INFLUENCING THE INFLUENCERS

In those days, middle-class women didn't work outside the home, but Susanna had a more-than-full-time job nonetheless. She dedicated herself selflessly to caring for her family. She ran the household, managed the finances (her husband was a poor money manager), and oversaw their modest farming efforts. Even when Samuel landed in debtors' prison at Lincoln Castle for three months, she persevered. And she did that while continuing to have numerous children, which was not unusual in those days. Over the course of twenty-one years, she gave birth to *nineteen* children, ten of whom survived.

Despite all the work that Susanna Wesley performed for her family, her most important task was to educate her children. For six hours every day (except Sunday), she dedicated herself to the moral and intellectual instruction of her three sons and seven daughters. She made it the object of her life.

When she was in her sixties, her son John asked her to share her methods by writing them down. Her reply:

> The writing anything about my way of education I am much averse to. It cannot, I think, be of service to anyone to know how I, who have lived such a retired life for so many years, used to employ my time and care in bringing up my children. No one can, without renouncing the world, in the most literal sense, observe my method; and there are few, if any, that would entirely devote above twenty years of the prime of life in hopes to save the souls of their children, which they think may be saved without so much ado; for that was my principal intention.[2]

She had performed an incredibly selfless act, and in the process, she had given up a lot—as she said, twenty years of her prime. But the results found in her children speak for themselves. Charles was an influential clergyman and has been called one of the greatest hymn writers of all time. And John is considered by many to have shaped England more than any other person of his generation. His impact on Protestant Christianity is still quite remarkable.

You may not be able to give your family the time that Susanna Wesley gave to hers. But what matters is that you give all you *can* to the people who are important to you. And you can do that only if you learn to get over yourself. Be more concerned with what you can give rather than what you can get because giving truly is the highest level of living.

Your Ninth Step to Failing Forward:

Get Over Yourself and Start Giving Yourself

If a selfish streak has been keeping you from getting over yourself, examine your attitude, and determine to make meeting the needs of others a priority in your life. You can start by asking yourself the following questions daily, either at the beginning or at the end of each day:

- Whom am I pouring my life into?
- Whom am I helping who cannot help me in return?
- Whom am I lifting who can't help himself?
- Whom am I encouraging daily?

If you will act with the interest of others in mind every day, you will soon be able to give concrete, affirming answers to these questions.

Steps to Failing Forward:

1. Realize there is one major difference between average people and achieving people.

2. Learn a new definition of *failure.*

3. Remove the "you" from failure.

4. Take action and reduce your fear.

5. Change your response to failure by accepting responsibility.

6. Don't let the failure from outside get inside you.

7. Say good-bye to yesterday.

8. Change yourself, and your world changes.

9. Get over yourself and start giving yourself.

Embracing Failure
As a Friend

10

Grasp the Positive Benefits of Negative Experiences

A failure is a man who blundered, but is not able to cash in on the experience.

—ELBERT HUBBARD

Working artists David Bayles and Ted Orland tell a story about an art teacher who did an experiment with his grading system for two groups of students. It is a parable on the benefits of failure. Here is what happened:

The ceramics teacher announced on opening day that he was dividing the class into two groups. All those on the left side of the studio, he said, would be graded solely on the *quantity* of work they produced, all those on the right solely on its *quality*. His procedure was simple: on the final day of class he would bring in his bathroom scales and weigh the work of the "quantity" group: fifty pounds of pots rated an "A," forty pounds a "B," and so on. Those being graded on "quality," however, needed to produce only one pot—albeit a perfect one—to get an "A." Well, came grading time and a curious fact emerged: the works of the highest quality were all produced by the group being graded for quantity. It seems that while the "quantity" group was busily churning out piles of work—and learning from their mistakes—the "quality" group had sat theorizing about perfection, and in the end had little more to show for their efforts than grandiose theories and a pile of dead clay.[1]

It doesn't matter whether your objectives are in the area of art, business, ministry, sports, or relationships. The only way you can get ahead is to fail early, fail often, and fail forward.

TAKE THE JOURNEY

I teach leadership to thousands of people each year at numerous conferences. And one of my deepest concerns is always that some people will go home from the event and nothing will change in their lives. They enjoy the "show" but fail to implement any of the ideas presented to them. I tell people continually: We overestimate the event and underestimate the process. Every fulfilled dream occurred because of dedication to a process. (That's one of the reasons I write books and create programs on audiocassette—so that people can engage in the ongoing *process* of growth.)

> *We overestimate the event and underestimate the process. Every fulfilled dream occurred because of dedication to a process.*

People naturally tend toward inertia. That's why self-improvement is such a struggle. But that's also why adversity lies at the heart of every success. The process of achievement comes through repeated failures and the constant struggle to climb to a higher level.

Most people will grudgingly concede that they must make it through some adversity in order to succeed. They'll acknowledge that they have to experience the occasional setback to make progress. But I believe that success comes only if you take that thought one step farther. To achieve your dreams, you must *embrace* adversity and make failure a regular part of your life. If you're not failing, you're probably not really moving forward.

THE BENEFITS OF ADVERSITY

Psychologist Dr. Joyce Brothers asserts, "The person interested in success has to learn to view failure as a healthy, inevitable part of the process of getting to the top." Adversity and the failure that often results from it should be expected in the process of succeeding, and they should be viewed as absolutely critical parts of it. In fact, the benefits of adversity are many. Consider these reasons to embrace adversity and persevere through it:

1. Adversity Creates Resilience

Nothing in life breeds resilience like adversity and failure. A study in *Time* magazine in the mid-1980s described the incredible resilience of a group of people who had lost their jobs three times because of plant closings. Psychologists expected them to be discouraged, but they were surprisingly optimistic. Their adversity had actually created an advantage. Because they had already lost a job and found a new one at least twice, they were better able to handle adversity than people who had worked for only one company and found themselves unemployed.[2]

> *To achieve your dreams, you must embrace adversity and make failure a regular part of your life. If you're not failing, you're probably not really moving forward.*

2. Adversity Develops Maturity

Adversity can make you better if you don't let it make you bitter. Why? Because it promotes wisdom and maturity. American playwright William Saroyan spoke to this issue: "Good people are good because they've come to wisdom through failure. We get very little wisdom from success, you know."

As the world continues to change at a faster and faster rate, maturity with flexibility becomes increasingly important. These qualities come from weathering difficulties. Harvard business school professor John Kotter says, "I can imagine a group of executives 20 years ago discussing a candidate for a top job and saying, 'This guy had a big failure when he was 32.' Everyone else would say, 'Yep, yep, that's a bad sign.' I can imagine that same group considering a candidate today and saying, 'What worries me about this guy is that he's never failed.'"[3] The problems we face and overcome prepare our hearts for future difficulties.

3. Adversity Pushes the Envelope of Accepted Performance

Lloyd Ogilvie told of a friend who was a circus performer in his youth. The fellow described learning to work on the trapeze:

> Once you know that the net below will catch you, you stop worrying about falling. You actually learn to fall successfully! What that means is, you can concentrate on catching the trapeze swinging toward you, and not on falling, because repeated falls in the past have convinced you that the net is strong and reliable when you do fall . . . The result of falling and being caught by the net is a mysterious confidence and daring on the trapeze. You fall less. Each fall makes you able to risk more.[4]

Until a person learns from experience that he can live through adversity, he is reluctant to buck mindless tradition, push the envelope of organizational performance, or challenge himself to press his physical limits. Failure prompts a person to rethink the status quo.

4. Adversity Provides Greater Opportunities

I believe that eliminating problems limits our potential. Just about every successful entrepreneur I've met has numerous stories of adversity and setbacks that opened doors to greater opportunity. For example, in 1978, Bernie Marcus, the son of a poor Russian cabinetmaker in Newark, New Jersey, was fired from Handy Dan, a do-it-yourself hardware retailer. That prompted Marcus to team with Arthur Blank to start their own business. In 1979, they opened their first store in Atlanta, Georgia. It was called The Home Depot. Today, The Home Depot has more than 760 stores employing more than 157,000 people, the business has expanded to include overseas operations, and each year the corporation does more than $30 billion in sales.

I'm sure Bernie Marcus wasn't very happy about getting fired from his job at Handy Dan. But if he hadn't been, who knows whether he would have achieved the success he has today.

5. Adversity Prompts Innovation

Early in the twentieth century, a boy whose family had immigrated from Sweden to Illinois sent twenty-five cents to a publisher for a book on photography. What he received instead was a book on ventriloquism. What did he do? He adapted and learned ventriloquism. The boy was Edgar Bergen, and for more than forty years he entertained audiences with the help of a wooden dummy named Charlie McCarthy.

The ability to innovate is at the heart of creativity—a vital component in success. University of Houston professor Jack Matson recognized that fact and developed a course that his students came to call "Failure 101." In it, Matson assigns students to build mock-ups of products that no one would ever buy. His goal is to get students to equate failure with innovation instead of defeat. That way they will free themselves to try new things. "They learn to reload and get ready to shoot again," says Matson. If you want to succeed, you have to learn to make adjustments to the way you do things and try again. Adversity helps to develop that ability.

6. Adversity Recaps Unexpected Benefits

The average person makes a mistake and automatically thinks that it's a failure. But some of the greatest stories of success can be found in the unexpected benefits of mistakes. For example, most people are familiar with the story of Edison and the phonograph: He discovered it while trying to invent something entirely different. But did you know that Kellogg's Corn Flakes resulted when boiled wheat was left in a baking pan overnight? Or that Ivory soap floats because a batch was left in the mixer too long and had a large volume of air whipped into it? Or that

Scott Towels were launched when a toilet paper machine put too many layers of tissue together?

Horace Walpole said that "in science, mistakes always precede the truth." That's what happened to German-Swiss chemist Christian Friedrich Schönbein. One day he was working in the kitchen—which his wife had strictly forbidden—and was experimenting with sulfuric acid and nitric acid. When he accidentally spilled

> *In science, mistakes always precede the truth.*
> —HORACE WALPOLE

some of the mixture on the kitchen table, he thought he was in trouble. (He *knew* he would experience "adversity" when his wife found out!) He hurriedly snatched up a cotton apron, wiped up the mess, and hung the apron by the fire to dry.

Suddenly there was a violent explosion. Evidently the cellulose in the cotton underwent a process called nitration. Unwittingly Schönbein had invented nitrocellulose—what came to be called smokeless gunpowder or guncotton. He went on to market his invention, which made him a lot of money.

7. Adversity Motivates

Years ago when Bear Bryant was coaching the University of Alabama's football team, the Crimson Tide was ahead by only six points in a game with less than two minutes remaining in the fourth quarter. Bryant sent his quarterback into the game with instructions to play it safe and run out the clock.

In the huddle, the quarterback said, "Coach says to play it safe, but that's what they're expecting. Let's give them a surprise." And with that, he called a pass play.

When the quarterback dropped back and threw the pass, the defending cornerback, who was a champion sprinter, intercepted the ball and headed toward the end zone, expecting to score a touchdown. The quarterback, who was not known as a good runner, took off after the cornerback and ran him down from behind, tackling him on the 5-yard line. His effort saved the game.

After the clock ran out, the opposing coach approached Bear Bryant and said, "What's this business about your quarterback not being a runner? He ran down my speedster from behind!"

Bryant responded, "Your man was running for six points. My man was running for his life."

Nothing can motivate a person like adversity. Olympic diver Pat McCormick discusses this point: "I think failure is one of the great motivators. After my narrow loss in the 1948 trials, I knew how really good I could be. It was the defeat that focused all my concentration on my training and goals." McCormick went on to win two gold medals in the Olympics in Helsinki in 1952 and another two in Melbourne four years later.

If you can step back from the negative circumstances facing you, you will be able to discover their positive benefits. That is almost always true; you simply have to be willing to look for them—and not take the adversity you are experiencing too personally.

If you lose your job, think about the resilience you're developing. If you try something daring and survive, evaluate what you learned about yourself—and how it will help you take on new challenges. If a bookstore gets your order wrong, figure out whether it's an opportunity to learn a new skill. And if you experience a train wreck in your career, think of the maturity it's developing in you. Besides, Bill Vaughan maintains that "in the game of life it's a good idea to have a few early losses, which relieves you of the pressure of trying to maintain an undefeated season." Always measure an obstacle next to the size of the dream you're pursuing. It's all in how you look at it.

WHAT COULD BE WORSE?

One of the most incredible stories of adversity overcome and success gained is that of Joseph, who was an ancient Hebrew. You may be familiar with the story. He was born the eleventh of twelve sons in a wealthy Middle Eastern family whose trade was raising livestock. As a teenager, Joseph alienated his brothers. First, he was his father's favorite, even though he was nearly the youngest. Second, he used to tell his father anytime his brothers weren't doing their work properly with the sheep. And third, he made the mistake of telling his older brothers that one day he would be in charge of them. Some of his brothers wanted to kill him, but the eldest, Reuben, prevented them from doing that. So when Reuben wasn't around, the others sold him into slavery.

Joseph ended up in Egypt working in the house of the captain of the guard, a man named Potiphar. Because of his leadership and administrative skills, Joseph quickly rose in the ranks, and before long, he was running the entire household. He was making the best of a bad situation. But then things got worse. The wife of his master tried to persuade him to sleep with her. When he refused, she accused *him* of making advances to *her* and got Potiphar to throw Joseph in prison.

FROM SLAVERY TO PRISON

At that point, Joseph was in a really difficult position. He was separated from his family. He was living in a foreign land. He was a slave. And he was locked in prison. But again, he made the best of a tough situation. Before long, the warden of the prison put Joseph in charge of all prisoners and the prison's daily activities.

Joseph met a fellow prisoner who had been an official in Pharaoh's court, the chief cupbearer. And Joseph was able to do him a favor by interpreting the man's dream. When he saw that the official was grateful, Joseph made a request of him in return.

"When all goes well with you," Joseph asked, "remember me and show me kindness; mention me to Pharaoh and get me out of this prison. For I was forcibly carried off from the land of the Hebrews, and even here I have done nothing to deserve being put in a dungeon."[5]

Joseph had hope a few days later when the official was returned to court and the good graces of the monarch. He expected any minute to receive word that Pharaoh was setting him free. But he waited. And waited. Two *years* passed before the cupbearer remembered Joseph, and he did so only because Pharaoh wanted someone to interpret his dreams.

FINALLY THE PAYOFF

In the end, Joseph was able to interpret Pharaoh's dreams. And because the Hebrew showed such wisdom, the Egyptian ruler put Joseph in charge of the entire kingdom. As the result of Joseph's leadership, planning, and system of food storage, when famine struck the Middle East seven years later, many thousands of people who otherwise would have died were able to survive, including Joseph's own family. When his brothers traveled to Egypt for relief from the famine—*twenty* years after selling him into slavery—they discovered that their brother Joseph was not only alive, but second in command of the most powerful kingdom in the world.

Few people would welcome the adversity of thirteen years in bondage as a slave and prisoner. But as far as we know, Joseph never gave up hope and never lost his perspective. Nor did he hold a grudge against his brothers. After their father died, he told them, "You intended to harm me, but God intended it for good to accomplish what is now being done, the saving of many lives." He found the positive benefits in his negative experiences. And if he can do it, so can we.

Your Tenth Step to Failing Forward:

Find the Benefit in Every Bad Experience

Finding the benefit in a bad experience is an ability that takes time to develop and effort to cultivate. You can start by thinking of the last major setback you experienced and listing all of the benefits that have occurred— or might occur—as a result. Do that now:

Major Setback:

Benefits That Occurred:
1.
2.
3.

Benefits That Might Occur:

1.

2.

3.

Once you've learned how to go through that process for an event from your past, the next step involves learning to do it *as* you experience adversity. During the coming week, as you experience problems, setbacks, or failures, take some time at the end of the day to brainstorm all the good things that can come of them. And try to maintain a positive mind-set as you move forward so that you can keep yourself open to the coming benefits of failure.

Steps to Failing Forward:

1. Realize there is one major difference between average people and achieving people.

2. Learn a new definition of *failure.*

3. Remove the "you" from failure.

4. Take action and reduce your fear.

5. Change your response to failure by accepting responsibility.

6. Don't let the failure from outside get inside you.

7. Say good-bye to yesterday.

8. Change yourself, and your world changes.

9. Get over yourself and start giving yourself.

10. Find the benefit in every bad experience.

11

Take a Risk—There's No Other Way to Fail Forward

While one person hesitates because he feels inferior,
the other is busy making mistakes and becoming superior.
—HENRY C. LINK

Every era has its great explorers, people willing to face danger to break new ground and discover new worlds. Americans love those kinds of people. The names of pioneers and daring adventurers ring throughout our history: Columbus, Crockett, Lewis and Clark, Lindbergh, Armstrong. The fuel that makes it possible for people like them to conquer new territory is risk. Pioneer aviator Charles Lindbergh emphasized that point: "What kind of man would live where there is no daring? I don't believe in taking foolish chances, but nothing can be accomplished if we don't take any chances at all."

Risk is a funny thing; it's very subjective. Here's what I mean: Someone may have no trouble plunging off a high tower with a bungee cord attached to his leg, but the same person may regard speaking in front of a group of twenty people as a death-defying risk. To another person, speaking isn't intimidating at all. For example, I love to speak to groups, and I've spoken to groups as large as eighty-two thousand people. On the other hand, I would never willingly bungee jump.

How do you judge whether some activity is worth the risk? Do you base it on your fear? No, you should do some things that scare you. Should you base it on the probability of success? No, I don't think that's the answer either. Risk must be evaluated not by the fear it generates in you or the probability of your success, but by the *value* of the goal.

> *Risk must be evaluated not by the fear it generates in you or the probability of your success, but by the value of the goal.*

SHE'S A PIONEER?

Allow me to tell you the story of someone who pushed the envelope of risk in order to achieve goals that were valuable to her. As she grew up, there were no significant indications that Millie would someday be one of the great adventurers of the twentieth century. She was an inquisitive child, born in Kansas in 1897. She was bright and excelled academically. She liked reading books and reciting poetry. She also enjoyed sports, particularly basketball and tennis.

After recognizing the impact of war on the soldiers who served in Europe during World War I, Millie wanted to do something to help. She decided to study nursing, and during the war, she worked as a military nurse's aide in Canada. After the war was over, she enrolled as a premed student at Columbia University in New York. In 1920, after her first year at school was finished, she visited her family in Los Angeles. That's when she took her first plane ride at Daugherty Field in Long Beach, California. And she was hooked. "As soon as we left the ground I knew I myself had to fly," she said.[1] She never returned to med school.

BOLD VENTURES

That was the beginning of a new life for Millie. Oh, I should mention that "Millie" is what her family called her. You and I know her as Amelia—

Amelia Earhart. She immediately began working odd jobs to earn the $1,000 required to take flying lessons, and soon she was learning how to fly from Anita Snook, another pioneer flier.

Learning to fly wasn't easy—at least not for Earhart. She had more than her share of crashes. But she persevered. Years later, she told her husband her perspective on flying: "Please know I am quite aware of the hazards . . . I want to do it because I want to do it. Women must try to do things as men have tried. When they fail, their failure must be but a challenge to others."[2]

In 1921, Earhart made her first solo flight. The next year she set the first of her many aviation records (for highest altitude). She piloted planes because she loved to fly, but she also had an agenda. She was trying to break ground for others. "My ambition is to have this wonderful gift produce practical results for the future of commercial flying and for the women who may want to fly tomorrow's planes," she said.[3]

During the course of her flying career, Earhart set many records and achieved many firsts:

- 1928: First woman to cross the Atlantic Ocean in an aircraft as passenger.
- 1929: First president of the Ninety-nines, an association of female pilots.
- 1930: Women's speed record of 181.8 miles per hour on a three-kilometer course.
- 1931: First person to set an altitude record in an autogiro (early helicopter) at 18,451 feet.
- 1932: First female pilot to fly solo over the Atlantic Ocean.
- 1935: First person to fly solo and nonstop between Oakland, California, and Honolulu, Hawaii.

ONE MORE BIG RISK

By 1935, Amelia Earhart was a seasoned, world-class pilot and had done a lot to accomplish her goals of opening doors for women and legitimizing commercial aviation. She must have believed the motto of all great achievers, "If at first you *do* succeed, try something harder," because that's when she decided to embark on her greatest adventure. She intended to fly around the world. That feat had already been accomplished by a man, but Earhart intended to route her flight near the equator and set a record for the longest flight (by either gender) at 29,000 miles.

In March 1935, she started on her way. She flew the first leg from Oakland to Hawaii. But as she took off from Luke Field near Pearl Harbor, she blew a tire and crashed the plane, causing tremendous damage. She had failed—but she wasn't ready to give up. Her plane was shipped to California for repairs, and she planned her next attempt.

Two years later, in June 1937, Earhart again started on her around-the-world voyage, this time heading east. She observed, "I have a feeling that there is just about one more good flight left in my system and I hope this trip is it. Anyway when I have finished this job, I mean to give up long-distance 'stunt' flying."[4] By the end of June, she and her navigator, Frederick Noonan, had flown 22,000 miles. When they took off from New Guinea on July 2, they were filled with hope because there were only 7,000 miles to go. But they were never seen again. Although U.S. Navy ships searched diligently, no trace of them or their plane was found.

WORTH THE RISK

If anyone had been able to talk to Earhart during her last hours, I believe she would not have expressed any regret for attempting what she did. She once said, "Now and then women should do for themselves what men have already done—occasionally what men have not done—thereby establishing themselves as persons, and perhaps encouraging other women toward greater independence of thought and action. Some such consideration was a contributing reason for my wanting to do what I so much wanted to do."[5]

To achieve any worthy goal, you must take risks. Amelia Earhart believed that, and her advice when it came to risk was simple and direct: "Decide whether or not the goal is worth the risks involved. If it is, stop worrying."

The reality is that *everything* in life is risky. If you want to avoid all risk, then don't do any of the following:

Don't ride in an automobile—they cause 20 percent of all fatal accidents.
Don't travel by air, rail, or water—16 percent of all accidents result from these activities.
Don't walk in the street—15 percent of all accidents occur there.
Don't stay at home—17 percent of all accidents happen there.[6]

In life, there are no safe places or risk-free activities. Helen Keller, author, speaker, and advocate for disabled persons, asserted, "Security is mostly a superstition. It does not exist in nature, nor do the children of men as a whole experience it. Avoiding danger is no safer in the long run than outright exposure. Life is either a daring adventure or nothing."

> *I do not believe in a fate that falls on men however they act; but I do believe in a fate that falls on them unless they act.*
> —*G. K. Chesterton*

Everything in life brings risk. It's true that you risk failure if you try something bold because you might miss it. But you also risk failure if you stand still and don't try anything new. G. K. Chesterton wrote, "I do not believe in a fate that falls on men however they act; but I do believe in a fate that falls on them unless they act." The less you venture out, the greater your risk of failure. Ironically the more you risk failure—and actually fail—the greater your chances of success.

When it comes to taking risks, I believe there are two kinds of people: those who don't dare try new things, and those who don't dare miss them.

Don't-Dare-Try-It People	Don't-Dare-Miss-It People
1. They *resist* opportunities.	1. They *find* opportunities.
2. They *rationalize* their responsibilities.	2. They *finish* their responsibilities.
3. They *rehearse* impossibilities.	3. They *feed* on impossibilities.

4. They *rain* on enthusiasm.

5. They *review* their inadequacies.

6. They *recoil* at the failure of others.

7. They *reject* the personal cost involved.

8. They *replace* goals with pleasure.

9. They *rejoice* that they have not failed.

10. They *rest* before they finish.

11. They *resist* leadership.

12. They *remain* unchanged.

13. They *replay* the problems.

14. They *rethink* their commitment.

15. They *reverse* their decision.

Motto: I would rather try nothing great and succeed than try something great and risk failure.

4. They *fan* the flame of enthusiasm.

5. They *face* their inadequacies.

6. They *figure* out why others failed.

7. They *finance* the cost into their lifestyle.

8. They *find* pleasure in the goal.

9. They *fear* futility, not failure.

10. They *finish* before they rest.

11. They *follow* leaders.

12. They *force* change.

13. They *fish* for solutions.

14. They *fulfill* their commitments.

15. They *finalize* their decision.

Motto: I would rather try something great and fail than try nothing great and succeed.

If you want to increase your odds of success, you have to take chances.

TRAPS THAT MAKE PEOPLE BACK AWAY FROM RISK

If risk has such great potential rewards, then why don't people embrace it as a friend? I believe they don't because they tend to fall into one or more of the following six traps:

1. The Embarrassment Trap

Deep down, nobody wants to look bad. And if you take a risk and fall flat on your face, you might embarrass yourself. So what? Get over it. The only way to become better is to take steps forward—even shaky ones that cause you to fall down. Little progress is better than no progress at all. Success comes in taking many small steps. If you stumble in a small step, it rarely matters. Don't gift wrap the garbage. Let little failures go.

2. The Rationalization Trap

> **Spend sufficient time confirming the need, and the need will disappear.**
> —ED'S FIFTH RULE OF PROCRASTINATION

People who are caught in the rationalization trap second-guess everything they do, and as they prepare to take action, they say to themselves, "Maybe it's really not that important." But the truth is, if you wait long enough, *nothing* is important. Or as Ed's Fifth Rule of Procrastination states, "Spend sufficient time confirming the need, and the need will disappear."

Sydney J. Harris says, "Regret for the things we did can be tempered by time; it is regret for the things we did not do that is inconsolable." If you take risks and fail, you'll have fewer regrets than if you do nothing and fail.

3. The Unrealistic Expectation Trap

For some reason, many people think everything in life should be easy, and when they find out that achievement takes effort, they give up. But success takes hard work.

Consider this Latin proverb: "If there is no wind, row." As you prepare to take a risk, don't expect to get a favorable wind. Begin with the mind-set that you have to row; then if you receive help, it will be a pleasant surprise.

> **If there is no wind, row.**
> —LATIN PROVERB

4. The Fairness Trap

When psychologist M. Scott Peck begins his book *The Road Less Traveled* with the words "Life is difficult" what he is getting at is life isn't fair. Many people never learn that fact. Instead of acknowledging it and moving on, they expend their energy trying to find fairness. They say to themselves, "I shouldn't have to be the one to do this."

Dick Butler expands on this idea: "Life isn't fair. It isn't going to be fair. Stop sniveling and whining and go out and make it happen for you." Wishing that a risk wasn't yours to take won't make it any easier. In fact, it might make it harder. Your attitude about it is your choice.

5. The Timing Trap

Don Marquis, the famous writer and humorist, was known to be a champion procrastinator. A friend who knew of this tendency in Marquis asked him how he ever got his day's work done. "That's simple," said Marquis. "I just pretend that it's yesterday's."

Some people tend to think that there's a perfect time to do everything—and this isn't it. So they wait. But Jim Stovall advises, "Don't wait for all the lights to be green before you leave the house." If you wait for perfect timing, you'll wait forever. And the more you wait, the more tired you'll get. William James wisely declared, "There is nothing so fatiguing as the eternal hanging on of an uncompleted task." Don't use timing as an excuse to procrastinate.

6. The Inspiration Trap

Someone once said, "You don't have to be great to start, but you have to start to be great." Many people want to wait for inspiration before they are willing to step out and take a risk. I find that's especially true of people with an artistic bent. But as playwright Oscar Wilde said, when he was asked the difference between a professional writer and an amateur, the difference is that an amateur writes when he feels like it; a professional writes regardless.

When it comes to moving forward, Bill Glass gives this advice: "When you get an insight or inspiration, do something about it in twenty-four hours—or the odds are against your ever acting on it."

ARE YOU TAKING ENOUGH RISKS?

As you examine the way you live, consider whether you are taking enough risks—not senseless ones, but intelligent ones. Even if you don't fall into one of the six traps I just reviewed, you still may be playing it too safe. How can you tell? By looking at your mistakes.

Fletcher L. Byrom says:

Make sure you generate a reasonable number of mistakes. I know that comes naturally to some people, but too many executives are so afraid of error that they rigidify their organization with checks and counterchecks, discourage innovation, and, in the end, so structure themselves that they will miss the kind of offbeat opportunity that can send a company skyrocketing. So take a look at your record, and if you can come to the end of a year and see that you haven't made any mistakes, then I say, brother, you just haven't tried everything you should have tried.

If you are succeeding in everything you do, then you're probably not pushing yourself hard enough. And that means you're not taking enough risks.

ANOTHER KIND OF RISK TAKING

You may have trouble relating to the great explorers and adventurers from history such as Amelia Earhart. The risks those people took may seem too different from your life situation. If so, you need to know about the life of someone whose quiet willingness to risk may seem more like your own.

His name was Joseph Lister, and he was a second-generation physician born in England in 1827. Back in the days when he began practicing medicine, surgery was a painful, grisly affair.

If you had the misfortune of being injured and requiring surgery in the mid-1800s, here's what you could have expected: You would have been taken to a hospital's surgical theater, a building that was separate from the main hospital to prevent the regular patients from becoming upset by the screaming. (Anesthesia had not yet been developed.) You would have been strapped to a table that looked a lot like the one in your kitchen, under which sat a tub of sand, positioned to catch blood.

Your surgery would have been performed by a physician or barber likely surrounded by a group of observers and assistants. All of them would be dressed in the regular street clothes they wore throughout the course of the day while traveling around town and treating patients. The instruments the doctor used would have been pulled from a nearby drawer where they had been placed (unwashed) after the previous surgery. And if your surgeon needed his hands free while working on you, he might have held the surgical knife between his teeth.

Your chances of surviving surgery would be a little better than 50 percent. If you had the misfortune of having your operation in a military hospital, your chances of surviving would go down to about 10 percent. Of surgery during that era, one contemporary doctor wrote, "A man laid on the operating table in one of our surgical hospitals is exposed to more chances of death than the English soldier on the field of Waterloo."[7]

DETERMINED TO MAKE A DIFFERENCE

Like the other surgeons of his time, Lister was distressed by the death rate of his patients, but he was ignorant of the cause. However, he was determined to discover a way to save more of his patients.

Lister's first major breakthrough came after he was given some writings by his friend Thomas Anderson, a chemistry professor. The papers were written by scientist Louis Pasteur. In them the French scientist stated his opinion that gangrene was caused not by air, but by bacteria and germs present in air. Lister thought those ideas were remarkable. And he theorized that if the dangerous microbes could be eliminated, his patients would have a better chance of avoiding gangrene, blood poisoning, and the other infections that often killed them.

INNOVATION MAKES HIM AN OUTCAST

Because of what we know today about germs and infection, Lister's ideas may seem to be common sense. But his belief was radical in those days—even among members of the medical community. And when Lister, who was working at a hospital in Edinburgh, presented his beliefs to the senior surgeons, he was taunted, ridiculed, and rejected. Each day as he made his rounds, his colleagues insulted and criticized him mercilessly. He was an outcast.

Despite the rejection of his peers and an inherently gentle nature, Lister refused to back down. He continued his work on the problem, but did his research at home. For a long time he and his wife worked in a laboratory they had created in their kitchen. The key, he believed, was to find a substance that would be capable of killing the microbes.

Lister finally settled on carbolic acid, a substance used to clean the sewage system in the city of Carlisle. His preliminary research done, he was ready to test his theory. But that would require another risk, one greater than rejection by his peers—he would have to experiment with carbolic acid on a living patient, not knowing whether it would kill him.

A GREATER RISK

Lister determined to wait until he found the right person. It would require someone who faced almost certain death. He found his patient on August 12, 1865. An eleven-year-old boy who had been run over by a cart was brought into the hospital. His leg had been so badly damaged that the broken bones had come through the skin. And his injury was more than eight hours old. He was the kind of patient who usually didn't survive.

Lister used carbolic acid to clean the wound, his instruments, and anything that came into contact with his patient. He also dressed the wound with bandages soaked in the substance. Then he waited. One day, two days, three days, then four days passed. To his joy, after four days there were no signs of fever or blood poisoning. After six weeks, the boy was able to walk again.

Amid heavy criticism, Lister used carbolic acid in all his procedures. During 1865 and 1866, he treated eleven patients with compound fractures, and none of his patients contracted infections. As he continued his new procedures, he did research to improve his methods, finding additional antiseptic substances that worked even better.

THE RESULT OF RISK

In 1867, Lister published his findings, and still the medical profession ridiculed him. For more than a decade, he communicated his findings and encouraged other doctors to adopt his practices. Finally in 1881, sixteen years after his first success with a patient, his peers at the International Medical Congress held in London recognized his advances. They called his work perhaps the greatest advance that surgery had ever made.[8] In 1883, he was knighted. In 1897, he was made a baron. Today, if you've had any kind of surgery, as I have, you owe Dr. Joseph Lister a debt of gratitude. His risk secured our safety.

Lister's risks may not look as flashy as those taken by someone like Amelia Earhart, but that doesn't matter. What he did brought great personal achievement to him and lasting benefits to others. He wasn't content with success as a doctor. He attempted something more difficult—and riskier. And that's what matters. You risk because you have something of value you want to achieve. That's just another part of failing forward.

Your Eleventh Step to Failing Forward:
If at First You Do Succeed, Try Something Harder

The willingness to take greater risks is a major key to achieving success, and you may be surprised that it can solve two very different kinds of problems.

First, if you've been hitting all the goals you set for yourself, then you need to increase your willingness to take chances. The road to the next level is always uphill, so you can't coast there.

Conversely, if you find yourself in a place where it seems that you don't achieve many of your goals, you may be playing it too safe. Once again, the answer is a willingness to take greater risks. (It's ironic that opposite ends of the spectrum come together in the area of risk.)

Think about the next big goal ahead of you. Write down your plan for reaching it. Then go over that plan to see whether you have included enough risks. If not, find parts of that process where you can push the envelope, take more chances, and increase your opportunity for success.

Steps to Failing Forward:

1. Realize there is one major difference between average people and achieving people.

2. Learn a new definition of *failure*.

3. Remove the "you" from failure.

4. Take action and reduce your fear.

5. Change your response to failure by accepting responsibility.

6. Don't let the failure from outside get inside you.

7. Say good-bye to yesterday.

8. Change yourself, and your world changes.

9. Get over yourself and start giving yourself.

10. Find the benefit in every bad experience.

11. If at first you do succeed, try something harder.

12

Make Failure Your Best Friend

The things which hurt, instruct.

—BENJAMIN FRANKLIN

The idea that you can make failure your best friend may seem odd to you. But the truth of the matter is that failure is either your friend or your enemy—and you are the one who chooses which it is. If you play a dirge every time you fail, then failure will remain your enemy. But if you determine to learn from your failures, then you actually benefit from them—and that makes failure your friend. If you repeatedly use your failures as springboards to success, then failure can become your *best* friend. Let me show you what I mean.

EMBRACING TRAGEDY

How would you feel about an incident that cost you your nose, half your right arm, and all the fingers on your left hand? I'm guessing that you wouldn't have positive feelings. But that's what happened to Dr. Beck Weathers, and he sees that loss as the defining event in his life—the event that turned everything around for him.

"Would I like to have my hands back?" he said in an interview on CBS Evening News. "Sure. Would I like to have my hands back enough to go back to who I was? No."

What event would cause a man to willingly *embrace* such a drastic disability? The answer can be found on Mount Everest. You see, Beck Weathers was one of the people on that peak during the now-famous incident in 1996 when a blizzard cost twelve people their lives.

NO ORDINARY MOUNTAINTOP EXPERIENCE

Weathers was forty-nine years old when he ascended Everest. At that point, he had been a mountain climber for ten years. And it consumed him. He acknowledges,

> I regret the time taken away from my family, from my wife and two children. There's a large dose of selfishness involved in such an activity . . . I realize I was defining myself by climbing and not dealing with the rest of my life. It's an excessive goal, and it never ends. You get about one day of happiness, and then you're planning your next trip.[1]

Weathers always spent a lot of time in preparation for his next trip. Before Everest, he had scaled six of the seven summits, the highest mountains on the continents. And for each climb he underwent a grueling training regimen.

For the Everest climb, Weathers signed on with an expedition led by New Zealander Rob Hall. Before the team got to the high camp (at twenty-six thousand feet), Weathers was doing fine, despite the difficult conditions—bitter cold and one-third of the oxygen present at sea level. But as he ascended the peak on May 10, Weathers realized he was in trouble. Some years before, he had undergone radial keratotomy surgery to correct his vision. As he went up the mountain, the altitude caused the lenses in his eyes to flatten out, and that made him blind.

LEFT FOR DEAD

At the time, the wisest decision seemed to be for Weathers to wait where he was, then rejoin the crew as they came back down from the summit. But Weathers's disappointment was soon overshadowed by nightmarish weather conditions. A freak blizzard rapidly enveloped the mountain, dropping the temperature to about fifty degrees below zero and increasing winds to seventy miles per hour. The storm made everyone scramble for survival. As that happened, Weathers was left behind on the mountain. Hours passed, and he lapsed into a hypothermic coma.

Fellow climbers searched for Weathers for hours. And early in the morning on May 11, they found him; he was covered with ice and barely breathing. They knew he would die, so they left him where he was, returned to camp, and radioed to his wife that he was dead.

No person has ever come out of a hypothermic coma and survived— except Beck Weathers. Somehow, he revived, got up, found his way, and staggered back into camp. His jacket was open, his face was black beyond recognition with frostbite, and his exposed right arm was marble-white and frozen upright in front of him.[2]

RESURRECTION!

Even after his miraculous return to camp, nobody thought Weathers would survive. But he kept pulling through. Back home in Dallas, he received medical attention. He underwent ten surgeries; they amputated the fingers on his left hand, amputated his right arm near the elbow, and reconstructed a new nose using tissue from other parts of his body.

Through it all, Weathers went through a radical learning process. He believes he traded his hands for something more valuable—lessons about himself, his values, and life. He admits,

> I'm probably a much happier person now having gone through what I've gone through. I have a different set of priorities. You never know who you are and what you are until you've really been tested. You gain a whole lot more from having failure kicked up from around your ears than success could ever teach you. [3]

Beck Weathers's attitude reflects more than just gratitude for surviving a tragedy that should have killed him. He displays a teachability that has allowed him to change his life for the better. He has failed forward by making hardship his best friend.

IT'S A MIND-SET

Fortunately you don't have to be left for dead on top of the world's highest mountain to become teachable and learn how to make failure your friend. You can do it from the safety of your own home. All it requires is the right attitude.

Your attitude toward failure determines your altitude after failure. Some people never understand that. For example, John H. Holiday, the founder and editor of the *Indianapolis News*, stormed out of his office one day in search of the person who had spelled *height* as *hight*. When a worker checked the original copy and explained that Holiday himself had been the one who did it, the editor's response was, "Well, if that's the way I spelled it, that has to be right." The paper misspelled the word his way for the next thirty years. As Louis Armstrong insightfully quipped, "There are some people that if they don't know, you can't tell them."

> *Your attitude toward failure determines your altitude after failure.*

Teachability is an attitude, a mind-set that says, "No matter how much I know (or think I know), I can learn from this situation." That kind of thinking can help you turn adversity into advantage. It can make you a winner even during the most difficult circumstances. Sydney Harris sums up the elements of a teachable mind-set: "A winner knows how much he still has to learn, even when he is considered an expert by others. A loser wants to be considered an expert by others before he has learned enough to know how little he knows."

Business author Jim Zabloski writes,

Contrary to popular belief, I consider failure a necessity in business. If you're not failing at least five times a day, you're probably not doing enough.

The more you do, the more you fail. The more you fail, the more you learn. The more you learn, the better you get. The operative word here is *learn*. If you repeat the same mistake two or three times, you are not learning from it. You must learn from your own mistakes and from the mistakes of others before you."[4]

The ability to learn from mistakes has value not just in business, but in all aspects of life. If you live to learn, then you will really learn to live.

How to Learn from Your Failures and Mistakes

William Bolitho distinguishes between a sensible person and a foolish one: "The most important thing in life is not to capitalize on our gains. Any fool can do that. The really important thing is to profit from your losses. That requires intelligence; and it makes the difference between a man of sense and a fool."

Anyone can make failure a friend by maintaining a teachable attitude and using a strategy for learning from failure. To turn losses into profits, ask the following questions every time you face adversity:

> *A winner knows how much he still has to learn, even when he is considered an expert by others. A loser wants to be considered an expert by others before he has learned enough to know how little he knows.*
>
> —SYDNEY HARRIS

1. What Caused the Failure: the Situation, Someone Else, or Self?

You cannot find out what you can do unless you do all you can to find out what went wrong. So that's where you need to start. If you no longer personalize failure, as I suggested in Chapter 3, then it becomes easier to sort things out.

Where did things break down? Were you in a no-win situation? Did another person create the problem? Did you make a mistake? When Beck

141

Weathers examined his Mount Everest experience after the fact, he determined he had made mistakes that led to his failure. He explained, "When you're up that far, you get high-altitude stupid."

Always begin the learning process by trying to identify the cause of a problem.

2. Was What Happened Truly a Failure, or Did I Just Fall Short?

You need to determine if what happened was really a failure. What you think is your fault may have been an attempt to fulfill unrealistic expectations. It doesn't matter whether you place them on yourself or someone else does; if a goal is unrealistic and you miss it, that is not a failure.

To give you a better perspective on this, let me tell you a story that President Reagan told before he left office. It's about *Three Musketeers* author Alexandre Dumas.

The novelist and a friend had a heated argument, and one challenged the other to a duel. Both Dumas and his friend were expert marksmen, and they feared that if they proceeded with the duel, both would die. So they decided to draw straws to determine which of them would shoot himself. Dumas picked the short straw.

> *A realist is an idealist who has gone through the fire and been purified. A skeptic is an idealist who has gone through the fire and been burned.*
> —WARREN WIERSBE

With a sigh, he picked up his pistol, walked into the library, and closed the door, leaving behind him a group of worried friends. After a few moments, the loud report of a pistol shot echoed from the library. His friends immediately charged into the room, and there stood Dumas with the pistol still smoking in his hand.

"An amazing thing just happened," said Dumas. "I missed."

As you examine your problems, try to be like Dumas: Don't allow an unrealistic expectation to kill you.

3. What Successes Are Contained in the Failure?

An old saying states, "The gem cannot be polished without friction, nor man perfected without trials." No matter what kind of failure you experience, there is always a potential jewel of success contained in it. Sometimes it may be difficult to find. But you can discover it if you're willing to look for it.

My friend Warren Wiersbe says, "A realist is an idealist who has gone through the fire and been purified. A skeptic is an idealist who has gone through the fire and been burned." Don't allow the fire of adversity to make you a skeptic. Allow it to purify you.

4. What Can I Learn from What Happened?

> *Adversity is the first path to truth.*
>
> —LORD BYRON

I enjoy reading the comic strip *Peanuts* by Charles Schulz. In one of my favorites, Charlie Brown is at the beach building a beautiful sand castle. As he stands back to admire his work, it is suddenly consumed by a huge wave. Looking at the smooth sand mound that had been his creation a moment before, he says, "There must be a lesson here, but I don't know what it is."

That's the way many people approach adversity. They are so consumed by the events that they become bewildered and miss the whole learning experience. But there is always a way to learn from failures and mistakes. Poet Lord Byron was right when he stated, "Adversity is the first path to truth."

Restaurateur Wolfgang Puck says, "I learned more from the one restaurant that didn't work than from all the ones that were successes." And success is something he knows a lot about. He owns five critically acclaimed restaurants in California—Spago, Chinois on Main, Postrio, the Eureka Brewery, and Granita—and he has also opened restaurants in Chicago, Las Vegas, and Tokyo.

It's difficult to give general guidelines about how to learn from mistakes because every situation is different. But if you maintain a teachable attitude as you approach the process and try to learn *anything* you can about what you could do differently, you will improve yourself. When a person has the right mind-set, every obstacle introduces him to himself.

5. Am I Grateful for the Experience?

One way to maintain a teachable mind-set is to cultivate an attitude of gratitude. And that's possible even in the face of a huge disappointment.

For example, American sprinter Eddie Hart missed a preliminary heat for the one-hundred-meter sprint in the 1972 Olympics in Munich. As a result, he lost his chance to win an individual gold medal. But his perspective on the experience was good. He said, "Everything you pursue you won't always attain. That's probably the most important lesson I learned from missing that race. There are times in life when you may not get the raise you want, the job you want. You have to learn to live with your defeats. And athletics are valuable, because they're all about winning and losing. Before you can actually be a good winner, you have to know how to lose."

Hart was grateful for the medal he received as a member of the relay team—and for the lesson it taught him about living with defeats. As you come away from a failure, try to cultivate a similar sense of gratitude.

6. How Can I Turn This into a Success?

Author William Marston writes, "If there is any single factor that makes for success in living, it is the ability to draw dividends from defeat. Every success I know has been reached because the person was able to analyze defeat and actually profit from it in the next undertaking."

Determining what went wrong in a situation has value. But taking that analysis another step and figuring out how to use it to your benefit is the real difference maker when it comes to failing forward. Sometimes the benefit comes from learning something that will help you avoid similar mistakes in the future. Other times it is a serendipitous discovery, such as

> *If there is any single factor that makes for success in living, it is the ability to draw dividends from defeat.*
> —WILLIAM MARSTON

Edison's phonograph or Schönbein's smokeless gunpowder. If you're willing to try, you can often salvage something of value from any disaster.

7. Who Can Help Me with This Issue?

People say there are two kinds of learning: experience, which is gained from your own mistakes, and wisdom, which is learned from the mistakes of others. I recommend that you learn from the mistakes of others as much as possible.

Learning from your failures is always easier with the help of a wise counselor. After making huge blunders, I've asked many people for advice: my dad, Jack Hayford, Elmer Towns, and my wife, Margaret (who is always willing to share her perspective of my blunders with me).

Seeking advice from the right person is important. I heard a story about a newly appointed public servant who was setting himself up in his new office. As he sat at his desk for the first time, he discovered that his predecessor had left him three envelopes along with instructions that they should be opened only in times of distress.

Before long, the man was in trouble with the press, so he decided to open the first envelope. The note said, "Blame your predecessor." So that's what he did.

For a while things went smoothly. But a few months later, he was in trouble again, so he opened the second envelope. The note said, "Reorganize." So that's what he did.

That bought him more time. But because he had never really resolved any of the issues that were causing him problems, he ended up in trouble again, and this time it was even greater than before. In desperation, he opened the last envelope.

The note inside read, "Prepare three envelopes."

Seek advice, but make sure it's from someone who has *successfully* handled his failures.

8. Where Do I Go from Here?

Once you've done all the thinking, you've got to figure out what to do next. In their book *Everyone's a Coach*, Don Shula and Ken Blanchard state,

"Learning is defined as a change in behavior. You haven't learned a thing until you can take action and use it."

MY OWN MOUNTAIN TO CLIMB

When you are able to learn from any bad experience and thereby turn it into a good experience, you make a major transition in life. For years I've taught something that I think gives useful insight on the subject of change:

> People change when they . . .
> Hurt enough that they have to,
> Learn enough that they want to, and
> Receive enough that they are able to.

I learned the truth of that statement on a whole new level on December 18, 1998. While at my company's Christmas party, I felt an excruciating pain in my chest, and I went down for the count. I suffered a serious heart attack. By the way, a mild heart attack is when it's yours; a serious heart attack is when it's mine! Honestly, though, I thought I wasn't going to make it that night. And my doctors later told me that if I'd had the experience four years ago, it would have killed me. Cardiologists didn't possess the technology that saved my life until very recently.

> *Learning is defined as a change in behavior. You haven't learned a thing until you can take action and use it.*
>
> —DON SHULA AND
> KEN BLANCHARD

WHAT I'VE GAINED

My heart attack was a painful and surprising experience, but I feel that God was very good to me in that process. Several excellent physicians rallied around me and made it possible for me not only to survive but also to avoid any permanent heart damage. And I've learned a lot from it, for example:

- When it comes to telling the important people in your life how much you love them, you can never do it often enough.

- I believe my work on earth is not yet finished and God has spared me so that I can complete it.

- I must change my living habits for the sake of my health, the quality of my life, and the impact I desire to make in the future.

My cardiologist, Dr. Marshall, told me that men who survive an early heart attack and learn from it live longer and healthier lives than those who never suffer a heart attack. I am determined to learn from the experience. I changed my diet.

> *Don't let your learning lead to knowledge; let your learning lead to action.*
>
> —*Jim Rohn*

I exercise every day and strive to live a more balanced life. Mark Twain's comment was true: "The only way to keep your health is to eat what you don't want, drink what you don't like and do what you'd rather not."

I have to admit that it's sometimes a struggle, but I'm persevering. As I write this, it has been over a year since the heart attack, and I have not cheated on my diet or exercise program. And I won't. The changes I've made are permanent. I've taken to heart Jim Rohn's comment: "Don't let your learning lead to knowledge; let your learning lead to action." I believe the action I'm taking now will enable me to enjoy my wife, children, and future grandchildren, and it will allow me to continue my mission for decades that I would have otherwise missed.

You don't need to suffer a heart attack or be caught in a blizzard on Mount Everest to make failure your best friend. All you have to do is to maintain a teachable heart and be eager to learn every time you fail.

Your Twelfth Step to Failing Forward:

Learn from a Bad Experience and Make It a Good Experience

Analyze a recent failure using the questions outlined in the chapter:

1. What caused the failure: the situation, someone else, or self?

2. Was what happened truly a failure, or did I just fall short?

3. What successes are contained in the failure?

4. What can I learn from what happened?

5. Am I grateful for the experience?

6. How can I turn this into a success?

7. Who can help me with this issue?

8. Where do I go from here?

Take the time to write down your conclusions, what you learned from your analysis, and any action you need to take to make your failure into a success. Share your observations with an adviser who can help you determine if your conclusions are on target.

Steps to Failing Forward:

1. Realize there is one major difference between average people and achieving people.

2. Learn a new definition of *failure.*

3. Remove the "you" from failure.

4. Take action and reduce your fear.

5. Change your response to failure by accepting responsibility.

6. Don't let the failure from outside get inside you.

7. Say good-bye to yesterday.

8. Change yourself, and your world changes.

9. Get over yourself and start giving yourself.

10. Find the benefit in every bad experience.

11. If at first you do succeed, try something harder.

12. Learn from a bad experience and make it a good experience.

Increasing Your Odds
for Success

13

Avoid the Top Ten Reasons People Fail

*Lord, deliver me from the man who never makes a mistake,
and also from the man who makes the same mistake twice.*

—DR. WILLIAM MAYO

I don't put much stock in the idea of luck. I think that usually things go well or not so well for people based on their actions. I believe that for the most part you create your own luck by working hard, practicing self-discipline, remaining persistent, and making personal growth a daily priority. Add to that the blessings of a loving God, and you don't need to think about luck.

However, a few years ago, I came across an article printed in the *Los Angeles Times* that almost made me change my mind about luck. Here's what it said:

NEW YORK—Jolted, jilted, hammered in a car crash and robbed, Lawrence Hanratty was named Friday as the unluckiest man in New York.

Nearly electrocuted in a construction site accident in 1984 that put him in a coma for weeks, Hanratty lost the lawyers fighting for his disability claim—one was disbarred, two died—and his wife ran off with her lawyer.

Hanratty, who has spent years fighting heart and liver disease, had his car wrecked in a crash last year. When police left the scene of the accident, he was held up and robbed.

"I say to myself, 'How much more am I going to be tested in life to see how much I can endure?'" Hanratty told the *New York Daily News* in a description of more than 10 years of agony that runs under the Page One headline: "Think You Got it Bad? Meet . . . Luckless Larry."

As if he hasn't tolerated enough hardship, 38-year-old Hanratty of Mt. Vernon, N.Y., said an insurance company now wants to cut off his workers' compensation benefits and his landlord has threatened to kick him out of his apartment.

Depressed and suffering from agoraphobia, a fear of open spaces, Hanratty uses a canister of oxygen and takes 42 pills a day for his heart and liver ailments. But with help from neighbors and a New York state assemblyman, he is not giving up yet.

"There's always hope," he said.[1]

Reading that story makes you want to try to find poor Lawrence to see if you can help him out in some way, doesn't it?

I think the experiences of Lawrence Hanratty are not typical of most people who continually fail or experience continual ongoing adversity. Why? Because most of the time the trouble we face is the result of our negative actions. It's our own fault.

THE TOP TEN WAYS PEOPLE GET IN THEIR OWN WAY

Many people possess blind spots when it comes to knowing about themselves. Sometimes the blind spots apply to strengths, but more often people fail to see their weaknesses. And that causes trouble. If you don't know you have a problem, then you can't work to fix it.

In the next several pages, I'd like to acquaint you with what I have observed to be the top ten reasons people fail. As you read, please be open-minded, and try to see yourself and your shortcomings in the following descriptions. Become aware of recurring issues in your life. As you read, you may find your Achilles' heel. By the way, the Achilles of ancient Greek myth was a warrior who was totally indestructible—except in one tiny spot on his heel. And that one flaw allowed his complete destruction. That's the way flaws work. So don't mentally minimize the amount of damage that a weakness may create.

1. Poor People Skills

By far the greatest single obstacle to success that I see in others is a poor understanding of people. A while back the *Wall Street Journal* printed an article on the reasons that executives fail. At the top of the list was a person's inability to effectively relate to others.

I was talking to some people a couple of days ago, and they were complaining about not winning a business contract that they had bid on. "It wasn't fair," one person told me. "All the people involved knew each other, and we didn't have a chance. It's all politics." But what he went on to describe wasn't politics. It was relationships.

Authors Carole Hyatt and Linda Gottlieb indicate that people who fail on the job commonly cite "office politics" as the reason for their failures, but the reality is that what they call politics is often nothing more than regular interaction with other people. Hyatt and Gottlieb assert,

> Most careers involve other people. You can have great academic intelligence and still lack social intelligence—the ability to be a good listener, to be sensitive toward others, to give and take criticism well.
>
> If people don't like you, they may *help* you fail . . . On the other hand, you can get away with serious mistakes if you are socially intelligent . . . A mistake may actually *further* [your] career if the boss thinks [you] handled the situation in a mature and responsible way.[2]

How are you when it comes to working with people? Are you genuine and authentic, or do you continually put up a front? Do you listen carefully to others, or do you do most of the talking? Do you expect everyone else to conform to your wishes, your schedule, and your agenda, or do you look for ways to meet people on their terms?

> *The most important single ingredient in the formula of success is knowing how to get along with people.*
> —THEODORE ROOSEVELT

If you haven't learned how to get along with people, you will always be fighting a battle to succeed. However, making people skills a strength will take you farther than any other skill you develop. People like to do business with people they like. Or to put it the way President Theodore Roosevelt did: "The most important single ingredient in the formula of success is knowing how to get along with people."

2. A Negative Attitude

I saw a cartoon that depicted a man getting his palm read by a fortune-teller. As she studied the man's palm, she said, "You will be sad, miserable, and poor until you're 30."

"Gee," the man replied hopefully, "what happens when I'm 30?"

The fortune-teller replied, "Then you'll get used to it."

Your reaction to the circumstances of your life has everything to do with your well-being and your success. W. Clement Stone tells a story about a young bride who traveled with her husband to the California desert during World War II.

Because she had grown up in the East, the desert seemed remote and desolate to her. Where they lived didn't make it any easier. The only housing they could find was a shack near a village of Native Americans, none of whom spoke English. She spent a lot of time there alone, waiting out the sweltering heat each day.

When her husband was gone for a long period, she wrote her mother to say she was returning home. A few days later, she received this reply:

Two men looked from prison bars,
One saw mud, the other stars.

Those words helped the young woman to see things more clearly. Maybe she couldn't improve her circumstances, but she could improve herself. She made friends with her Native American neighbors, she began working with them on weaving and pottery, and she took time to explore the desert and discover its natural beauty. All of a sudden, she was living in a new world—and the only thing that had changed was her attitude.

If your circumstances constantly get you down, then maybe it's time for a change—not in your situation, but in your attitude. If you can learn to make the best of any situation, you can remove a formidable obstacle that stands between you and your dreams.

3. A Bad Fit

Though we should always first examine our attitudes when we don't enjoy our circumstances, sometimes a change in situation is also in order. Sometimes a case of mismatched abilities, interests, personality, or values can be a major contributor to chronic failure.

A good example can be seen in the life of film producer David Brown. He started out in corporate America and was fired from three different jobs before he realized that corporate life was not for him. After working his way up in Hollywood and becoming the number two man at Twentieth Century Fox, he was fired after recommending a film that turned out to be a flop. Then he became an editorial vice president at the New American Library, but he was fired when he clashed with a coworker. Later he was rehired by Twentieth Century Fox, but six years later was fired again, along with Fox's president, Richard Zanuck.

Brown examined his working behavior and determined that his outspoken, risk-oriented ways didn't fit well in the settings where he had been working. He was too much of an entrepreneur to work in jobs with confining expectations. Although he had failed as a corporate executive, he was extremely successful when he pursued his own ideas with his former boss, Zanuck. He and Zanuck went on to produce many popular films, including the huge box office hit *Jaws*.

Few things in life are more frustrating than being stuck in a profession or organization that doesn't suit you. It's like always having to wear shoes that are two sizes too large or too small. Are you a salesperson stuck in an accountant's job? Are you a corporate executive who would rather be home raising your children? Are you an engineer who would rather be pastoring a church? Are you an entrepreneur working for an organization whose idea of progress is moving backward slowly? Evaluate yourself and your situation. If there is a poor fit, think about making a change.

4. Lack of Focus

Bad things happen when a person doesn't focus. Let me illustrate with a story. One day a businessman visited a small-town florist shop to order flowers for a friend who was opening a new business. The floral shop owner was unusually busy and was scrambling to fill orders while she took the businessman's information.

Later that day, the man arrived at his friend's grand opening and saw a big floral wreath with his name on it that said, "With Deepest Sympathy During This Time of Sorrow."

The businessman was irate. He called the florist to complain and asked, "What in the world happened? Do you have any idea how stupid you made me look?"

"I'm so sorry," the shop owner said, "I was a little scrambled when you came by. But your situation wasn't nearly as bad as it was at the funeral home. That card said, 'Best Wishes in Your New Location.'"

Anybody can make an honest mistake when things are hectic. But people lacking focus have trouble not because they're too busy, but because their priorities are out of whack. And that wastes their time and resources. If you go from task to task to task without making any progress, or you can't seem to reach a goal no matter how much effort you give it, examine your focus. No one can move forward without it.

5. A Weak Commitment

For a long time, it seemed that apathy was chic. But effort and commitment seem to be coming back into style. And that's good because without commitment, you cannot accomplish anything of value. Johann Wolfgang von Goethe addressed the importance of commitment: "Until one is committed, there is hesitance, the chance to draw back, and always ineffectiveness . . . The moment one definitely commits oneself . . . a whole stream of events issue from the decision, raising in one's favor all manner of unforeseen incidents and material assistance which no man could have dreamed would come his way."

The last time you failed, did you stop trying because you failed, or did you fail because you stopped trying? What was your level of commitment? Did you give the task everything you had? Did you go the extra mile? Did you put enough of yourself on the line to guarantee that you would give your very best?

If you're committed, a failure doesn't mean that you'll never succeed. It just means you will take longer. Commitment makes you capable of failing forward until you reach your goals.

6. An Unwillingness to Change

Perhaps the most relentless enemy of achievement, personal growth, and success is inflexibility. Some people seem to be so in love with the past that they can't deal with the present.

Not long ago, a friend sent me "The Top Ten Strategies for Dealing with a Dead Horse." I thought the list was hilarious:

1. Buy a stronger whip.

2. Change riders.

3. Appoint a committee to study the horse.

4. Appoint a team to revive the horse.

5. Send out a memo declaring the horse isn't really dead.

6. Hire an expensive consultant to find "the real problem."

7. Harness several dead horses together for increased speed and efficiency.

8. Rewrite the standard definition of *live horse*.

9. Declare the horse to be better, faster, and cheaper when dead.

10. Promote the dead horse to a supervisory position.

I bet you've seen just about every one of these "solutions" enacted in your place of work. But there's really only one effective way to deal with that problem: When your horse is dead, for goodness' sake, dismount.

One *Calvin and Hobbes* comic strip portrayed the way that too many of us perceive change. Calvin and his stuffed-tiger friend were speeding down a hill in the boy's wagon. Calvin yelled back to Hobbes, "I thrive on change."

Surprised, Hobbes remarked, "You? You threw a fit this morning because your mom put less jelly on your toast than yesterday."

Calvin faced Hobbes and explained, "I thrive on making other people change."

You don't have to love change to be successful, but you need to be willing to accept it. Change is a catalyst for personal growth. It gets you out of a rut, it gives you a fresh start, and it affords you an opportunity to reevaluate your direction. If you resist change, you're really resisting success. Learn flexibility, or learn to like living with your failures.

7. A Shortcut Mind-Set

A common obstacle to success is the desire to cut corners and take the short road to success. But shortcuts never pay off in the long run. As Napoleon said, victory belongs to the most persevering.

> *The common denominator of success lies in forming the habit of doing things that failures don't like to do.*
>
> —ALBERT GRAY

Most people tend to underestimate the time it takes to achieve something of value, but to be successful, you have to be willing to pay your dues. James Watt spent twenty years laboring to perfect his steam engine. William Harvey labored night and day for eight years to prove how blood circulated in the human body. And it took another twenty-five years for the medical profession to acknowledge he was right.

Cutting corners is really a sign of impatience and poor self-discipline.

But if you are willing to follow through, you can achieve a breakthrough. That's why Albert Gray says, "The common denominator of success lies in forming the habit of doing things that failures don't like to do."

If you continually give in to your moods or impulses, then you need to change your approach to doing things. The best method is to set standards for yourself that *require* accountability. Suffering a consequence for not following through helps you stay on track. Once you have your new standards in place, work according to them, not your moods. That will get you going in the right direction.

Self-discipline is a quality that is won through practice. Psychologist Joseph Mancusi noted, "Truly successful people have learned to do what does not come naturally. Real success lies in experiencing fear or aversion and acting in spite of it."

8. Relying on Talent Alone

Talent is overrated. Not because it doesn't have value, but because talent alone isn't enough to take a person through the multiple failures that life brings. Adding a strong work ethic to talent is like pouring gasoline on a fire. It's explosive!

The great artists understand this, though some nonartists mistakenly believe that talent alone carries them through. David Bayles and Ted Orland explain,

> Even at best, talent remains a constant, and those who rely upon that gift alone, without developing further, peak quickly and soon fade to obscurity. Examples of genius only accentuate that truth. Newspapers love to print stories about five-year-old musical prodigies giving solo recitals, but you rarely read about one going on to become a Mozart. The point here is that whatever his initial gift, Mozart was also an artist who learned to work on his work, and thereby improved. In that respect he shares common ground with the rest of us.[3]

The greater your talent, the more likely you are to lean heavily on it and skip the hard day-to-day work of improving it. If you possess this negative tendency, put yourself on a growth plan so that you can make the most of your God-given talent.

9. A Response to Poor Information

Successful executives have in common the ability to make weighty decisions based on limited amounts of information. But they also have in common the ability to gather reliable information to use as they evaluate issues. General Douglas MacArthur knew this. He asserted, "Expect only 5 percent of an intelligence report to be accurate. The trick of a good commander is to isolate the 5 percent."

As the pace of life and business increases, the difficulty of being able to collect and evaluate information will increase. In fact, Bill Gates's best-selling book *Business @ the Speed of Thought* was written specifically to address this issue.

An example of what can go wrong when decisions are made on the basis of poor information is evident in the purchase of Rolls-Royce Motor Cars. Volkswagen and BMW battled each other to purchase Rolls-Royce from Vickers PLC. And Volkswagen won the battle, paying $780 million for the luxury auto-making company. But after the purchase was finalized, the buyers made a shocking discovery. Volkswagen owned the company, but not the rights to the name Rolls-Royce, which is synonymous with luxury cars around the world. The license for the name, it turned out, belonged to another company: Rolls-Royce PLC, an aerospace company. Even worse, Rolls-Royce PLC had ties to BMW. Guess who received permission to use the name? BMW—not Volkswagen. And it all happened because of poor information gathering.

10. No Goals

The last major cause of failure is an absence of goals. Don Marquis perceives that "ours is a world where people don't know what they want and are willing to go through hell to get it."

Joe L. Griffith believes, "A goal is nothing more than a dream with a time limit." Many people don't have goals because they haven't allowed themselves to dream. As a result, they don't possess a desire. If that

> *Ours is a world where people don't know what they want and are willing to go through hell to get it.*
> —DON MARQUIS

describes you, then you must look deep within yourself and try to determine why you're on this planet. Once you've discovered that, you'll know what to shoot for. (I'll talk more about this in the next chapter.)

If you can discover the weakness that weakens you, then you can start doing something about it. And that can change your life. I've seen that happen again and again in people who desire success. Let me tell you about one of them.

PUTTING PURPOSE BEFORE PEOPLE

One of the people I rely on most at The INJOY Group is my good friend Dan Reiland. He and I have worked together for seventeen years. For more than a decade Dan was my right hand at Skyline Church, serving as my executive pastor. I couldn't have succeeded without him. When I resigned from the pastorate to lead The INJOY Group full-time, I took him with me. Today, he serves as INJOY's vice president of leadership development and church growth.

To say that Dan is naturally purpose driven would be an understatement. He is highly organized, and he goes after a goal with a vengeance. When I first met him, if he had dropped his briefcase and it had broken open, the contents would have fallen out in alphabetical order. But as is the case with many people, Dan's strength was also his weakness. Let's just say that because he was purpose driven, he was not the most relational guy in the world.

GOING RIGHT PAST HIS WORK

Initially Dan held the position of intern. I remember one day soon after he started the job, I was standing in the office lobby having a conversation with a group of people, and Dan came in from the parking lot with his carefully arranged briefcase. He walked right through the group of us and didn't say a word. He strode down the hall directly to his office.

I excused myself from the group, and I followed him. Dan set his briefcase down on his desk, and when he turned around, he was surprised to see that I was standing there.

"Dan," I said, "what are you doing? You walked right by us, and you didn't say anything."

"Well, I have a lot of work to do," Dan answered, pulling out a stack of papers.

"Dan," I said looking him in the eye, "you just passed your work." I wanted him to understand that people come first to a leader.

MAKING CHANGES

For the next year, Dan and I worked together, and I mentored him in the area of people skills. Dan worked especially hard; he was dedicated to improving himself. And you know, every year he got better. Today, if you were to meet Dan, you would think that his ability to work with people is a natural strength because he is so good at it. He is now one of the finest pastoral leaders in the country. And if I have a tricky assignment that requires someone with exceptional people skills to carry it out, do you know who is on my short list of choices? Dan. And that has become possible because of his willingness to grow and change. He has taken a weakness and turned it into a strength.

If you are dedicated to overcoming failure and achieving lasting success, then you need to be willing to do the same. Work on the weakness that weakens you, and there's no telling how far you will go.

Your Thirteenth Step to Failing Forward:

Work on the Weakness That Weakens You

Everybody has weaknesses. Review the top ten reasons people fail, and determine whether you need to work on one of these areas. (Or you may have a different issue that isn't listed there.)

Start improving yourself by talking to a trusted friend. Ask him to help you evaluate yourself in your area of weakness. Then put yourself on a growth plan to turn that weakness into a strength. The plan may include reading books, attending classes or seminars, or finding a mentor. Determine to put your plan into action, and stick with it for *a year*.

At the end of that time, go back to the friend who helped you evaluate yourself, and ask the person to evaluate your progress. If you still need improvement, begin a second phase of growth, following it as long as you must to keep growing.

Steps to Failing Forward:

1. Realize there is one major difference between average people and achieving people.

2. Learn a new definition of *failure*.

3. Remove the "you" from failure.

4. Take action and reduce your fear.

5. Change your response to failure by accepting responsibility.

6. Don't let the failure from outside get inside you.

7. Say good-bye to yesterday.

8. Change yourself, and your world changes.

9. Get over yourself and start giving yourself.

10. Find the benefit in every bad experience.

11. If at first you do succeed, try something harder.

12. Learn from a bad experience and make it a good experience.

13. Work on the weakness that weakens you.

14

The Little Difference Between Failure and Success Makes a Big Difference

*There is no failure except no longer trying. There is no defeat
except from within, no really insurmountable barrier save
our own inherent weakness of purpose.*

—KEN HUBBARD

Most unsuccessful people believe that a huge gaping chasm stands between them and success. They suspect deep down that they will never be able to cross that void and get to the other side in achieving their dreams. But I want to let you in on a little secret. There's not much difference between failure and success, and the little difference makes a big difference. What creates that difference? Let me share a story with you, and you will be able to guess what the difference maker is.

THE START OF AN UPHILL BATTLE

I think everybody in the United States has heard of Macy's department store, thanks to its famous Thanksgiving Day parade and the movie *Miracle on 34th Street*. But fewer people know about the man who founded the store in 1858. His name was R. H. Macy.

The son of a sea captain, Macy was born in Nantucket at a time when whaling was king. His first job was on a whaling ship at age fifteen. He spent four years on that ship and saw the world, traveling as far as New Zealand. When he returned to the United States with his share of the ship's earnings, which amounted to $500, he was finished with the sea. He worked several odd jobs and then took a position as an apprentice in a printing shop. But he lasted only six months there. He had greater ambition than the printing trade offered.

A Venture into Retail

That's when he decided to try his hand at retail trade. With the money he had saved from his time at sea, he opened a small thread and needle store in Boston. His hopes were high, and his work ethic was strong, but the business failed within a year.

The next year, Macy tried again. His second store traded in dry goods, mainly European-made items bought at auction. Again he worked hard, and again he failed. The following year, he decided to team with his brother-in-law, Samuel S. Houghton, who eventually founded Houghton and Dutton in Boston. He worked with him and learned a lot, but after a year, he decided that he needed a change.

Go West, Young Man?

R. H. Macy and his brother Charles had heard about the gold strike in California, and they decided to head west and try their hands at mining. Though they failed to strike it rich, they immediately recognized that there were opportunities to make money selling goods to the miners. Along with two other partners, they opened Macy and Company in Marysville, a town north of Sacramento. And they did fairly well—until the gold ran out and the miners left the area. So they sold their business to a competitor and moved back east.

Macy's next venture was a dry goods store in Haverhill, Massachusetts, a town north of Boston. He had learned something from each business he had run, and he was starting to formulate a unique philosophy of trade. At his newest store, Macy introduced innovations that would later become his trademark: selling at a fixed price while other stores haggled, buying and selling for cash only, and advertising heavily. He even wrote his own copy and designed the layout for each ad, drawing on his time in the printing business.

Unfortunately he couldn't make it in that business either, so he closed its doors. He wasn't defeated, though. The following year, he opened another store, and he sold goods for the lowest prices in town. Yet despite his innovations, his clever advertising, and his hard work, that business didn't make it. After three years of struggle in a relatively small town, Macy sold out and declared bankruptcy.

MAKING A CHANGE

At that point Macy decided to get out of retail. For a while he worked as a stockbroker, then as a real estate broker. He moved to Wisconsin to pursue an opportunity, but a financial panic that year dashed his hopes of making it really big.

Despite the difficult times, he achieved modest success, and he was able to make some money. With Macy's big opportunity in Wisconsin having fallen through, a friend convinced him to give the retail trade another try. Once again, he returned to the West.

He had tried five professions—whaler, retailer, gold miner, stockbroker, and real estate broker. And this would be his *seventh* attempt in retail. He must have been weary, yet he was only thirty-five years old.

He decided to try his luck in Manhattan. And that was to make a tremendous difference. Even then New York was the largest city in the United States, and with a population of 950,000 was one hundred times larger than the Haverhill area. And New York was still growing. In 1858, R. H. Macy opened a fancy dry goods store. After only twelve months, he was grossing $80,000 a year. By the 1870s, the store averaged more than $1 million in sales per year.

THE FATHER OF RETAIL AS WE KNOW IT

As Macy's business grew, he revolutionized retail trade. He can be credited with numerous innovations:

- Inventing the concept of the modern department store
- Making set prices the norm in the industry instead of haggling
- Buying and selling in high volume in order to provide lower prices for customers
- Introducing modern retail advertising
- Appointing the first female executive in retail history

In 1877, Macy died while on a buying trip in Europe. However, his business lived on—and it continued to bring innovation to retail trade. Today, the company serves customers with 191 Macy's stores. Those stores exist because of one man who refused to give up.

THE POWER OF PERSISTENCE

As you have no doubt guessed, the quality that took Macy through failure after failure after failure was his persistence. That is the little difference that makes a big difference when it comes to failing forward. It separates those who achieve success from those who only dream about it.

Nothing worth achieving comes easily. The only way to fail forward and achieve your dreams is to cultivate tenacity and persistence. These qualities can be learned, partly by developing the habit of following through on your commitments when you don't feel like it. But to begin cultivating these qualities, you need a strategy. And that's what I want to give you now—a four-point plan for

> *More than anything else, what keeps a person going in the midst of adversity is having a sense of purpose. It is the fuel that powers persistence.*

approaching achievement that will encourage stamina and resilience in the face of failures.

1. *Purpose: Find One*

More than anything else, having a sense of purpose keeps a person going in the midst of adversity. It is the fuel that powers persistence.

Business consultant Paul Stoltz did an extensive study on what it takes for individuals to persist through setbacks. According to Stoltz, the most important ingredient of persistence is this:

> *Always bear in mind that your resolution to succeed is more important than any other thing.*
> —ABRAHAM LINCOLN

Identifying your mountain, your purpose in life, so that the work you do is meaningful. I run into people every day who are basically climbing the wrong mountain. People who have spent 20 years or more of their lives doing something that has no deep purpose for them. Suddenly they look back and go, "What have I been doing?"[1]

If you are a purpose-driven person naturally, then you probably already possess an innate sense of direction that helps you overcome adversity. But if you're not, then you may need some help. Use the following steps to help you *develop a desire.*

- Get next to people who possess great desire.

- Develop discontent with the status quo.

- Search for a goal that excites you.

- Put your most vital possessions into that goal.

- Visualize yourself enjoying the rewards of that goal.

If you follow this strategy, you may not immediately find your ultimate purpose, but you will at least start moving in that direction. And that's important. As Abraham Lincoln said, "Always bear in mind that your resolution to succeed is more important than any other thing." That resolution comes from a sense of purpose.

2. Excuses: Eliminate Them

Agricultural scientist George Washington Carver noted, "Ninety-nine percent of failures come from people who have the habit of making excuses." Having desire alone will not get you through your failures. You have to forget about making excuses and keep moving forward, as R. H. Macy did.

Recently I read a story about Dean Rhodes, a man who missed opportunity after opportunity. But he didn't make excuses for his shortcomings or whine about what might have been. He kept going. Here's what I mean. Rhodes met Dave Thomas long before the restaurateur opened his first Wendy's. Rhodes admitted that he always knew the young Thomas would "someday do something big." But when given the opportunity to invest in Wendy's, he didn't.

Later, Rhodes met Colonel Sanders and had an opportunity to buy stock in his company before it went national. But he turned that down as well because he didn't agree with some of the colonel's ideas.

When Rhodes was in the restaurant equipment business, he often had equipment salesmen in his office trying to sell him on their machines. One of them was Ray Kroc. Rhodes admitted that Kroc was a pleasant person. However, he chose not to invest in the little hamburger stand called McDonald's.

A few years later, on a cruise, he met an attorney from the Pacific Northwest who suggested that Rhodes invest in his son's new computer company. It had a funny name: Microsoft. Rhodes declined.

> *Effort only fully releases its reward after a person refuses to quit.*
>
> —NAPOLEON HILL

Most people would pull their hair out and complain if they missed only one of those opportunities, making excuses for why it didn't work out. Not Rhodes. He saw his mistakes for what they were and focused on pursuing his own dreams and opportunities. Eventually he saw his name at

#289 on the *Forbes* list of the 400 most successful business owners in America. No matter how many opportunities you've missed or mistakes you've made, don't ever make excuses. Bite the bullet, take complete responsibility for yourself, and keep trying.

3. Incentives: Develop Some

Nothing helps a person remain tenacious like a good incentive. That's why so many companies use them with their employees. Walter Elliot said, "Perseverance is not a long race; it is many short races, one after another." If you give yourself worthwhile incentives to win the short races, attaining a long-term goal seems less formidable.

As you develop incentives for yourself, keep these things in mind:

• Reward yourself only *after* you reach the goal.

• Divide the process into stages to multiply the rewards.

• Include others—that increases accountability and makes achievement more enjoyable.

What you choose to use as incentives is up to you. But match the incentive to the goal. Just as a parent doesn't reward a child for finishing his vegetables with a trip to Disneyland, don't make rewards for the small objectives too big. Otherwise you will undermine your desire to keep going.

4. Determination: Cultivate It

Author Napoleon Hill noted, "Effort only fully releases its reward after a person refuses to quit." To develop persistence over the long haul, you have to cultivate inward determination on a continual basis. And if you do, someday your story may be similar to one of these:

Admiral Peary attempted to reach the North Pole seven times before he made it on try number eight.

Oscar Hammerstein had five flop shows that lasted less than a combined total of six weeks before *Oklahoma*, which ran for 269 weeks and grossed $7 million.

John Creasey received 743 rejection slips from publishers before one word was ever published—he eventually published 560 books, which have sold more than 60 million copies.

Eddy Arcaro lost 250 consecutive races before he won his first.

Albert Einstein, Edgar Allan Poe, and John Shelley were all expelled from school for being mentally slow.

Learn to become a determined individual. Inspire yourself with stories of people who tried, failed, and kept going. And remember, the only difference between a little shot and a big shot is that the big shot kept shooting.

A Surprise at Christmas

I will always associate persistence with someone I got to know in San Diego about ten years ago while I was the senior pastor of Skyline Church. I first met him at a performance of our Christmas production. Those performances were always major events. Each year we did twenty-four performances over three weeks to audiences totaling more than twenty thousand people.

As I was backstage talking to some of the singers and actors before a performance, I heard them excitedly talking to one another.

"Orval's here. Orval is in the audience," I could hear them saying. I thought that was nice. Orval Butcher was the founding pastor of Skyline, and I was glad to see that the people were excited about putting on a good show for him.

When I stepped out in front of the people in the auditorium to welcome them to the performance, I spotted someone sitting in the front row that I recognized. He was a tall, thin man with wavy gray hair, glasses, suspenders, and a red bow tie. That's when I realized that they hadn't been talking about Orval Butcher—like me, they had seen Orville Redenbacher in the audience!

You'd Never Guess from Looking at Him

Over the years, I got to know Orville Redenbacher. He was bright and cheerful, just as he appeared to be on his television commercials. And he was generous too. About twice a year, a truck would pull up to my house, and the men would unload boxes of popcorn for me and my family—a gift from Orville.

Most people who saw Orville Redenbacher on television thought he was an actor portraying a businessman. He seemed so quirky that people assumed that his persona was a made-up character. *Adweek* described him as "a wry caricature sprung from 'American Gothic,' an owlish codger with the deportment of a life-long prom chaperone." But he was the genuine article. He personally developed the popcorn he sold, and how he did it is a study in persistence.

INDIANA FARM BOY

Redenbacher was born on a farm in Jackson Township, a few miles south of Brazil, Indiana, in 1907. At age twelve, he started growing popcorn in addition to doing his numerous chores. In time, his additional crop brought in $150 a month, most of which he set aside for college.

In 1924, he graduated from high school, the first person in his family to reach that milestone. He received an appointment to West Point, but instead he went to Purdue. His ambition was to become a county agent. Times were tough, and coming from a farming family meant that he didn't have much money. So Redenbacher worked hard and did lots of odd jobs for the university in the agriculture department, including some experiments with popcorn hybrids. Many times he considered quitting, but he always persevered. In a letter to his fiancée, he wrote why he hadn't given up:

> First, I always wanted my children to know I was a college graduate . . . Second, I was afraid people back home would think I couldn't make my grades, or else got kicked out and the third reason was because I told my folks that I was going to college . . . The first two summers I went home with the full intention of quitting, but these other things got to working and every fall found me back at Purdue.

In 1928, he received his degree in agriculture.

New Opportunities

The first job Redenbacher took was as a teacher. But the next year he became a county agent, a job he held until 1940 when he received an offer from the Princeton Mining Company to manage its newly acquired Princeton Farms. At twelve thousand acres it was the largest farm in Indiana. There he again experimented with popcorn hybrids.

For ten years Redenbacher managed Princeton's concerns and was highly successful. But in 1950, he and his friend Charlie Bowman decided to go into business together, purchasing the George F. Chester & Son Seed Company. Once again, Redenbacher was highly successful, and again, he spent lots of time developing his hybrid. To give you an idea of the magnitude of that task, read the words of his grandson, Gary Redenbacher:

> Grandpa was a tireless worker. The effort that was required to come up with the gourmet hybrid was enough work for anyone's lifetime. Those who have ever tried to hybridize a rose, or any other plant, know that it's just a matter of dogged determination and time. I tell people to imagine that they are in a football stadium full of fans. Imagine that each fan is a stalk of corn. Your job is to go to each cornstalk in the stands and individually pollinate each one. But since the average football stadium only holds about fifty thousand people, you'll need to do three stadiums before you've pollinated as many cornstalks as Grandpa did *each year* . . . Through all these tens of thousands of hybrids, Grandpa never lost sight of his goal: To produce a better popcorn. (Emphasis added)

Success at Last?

Finally, in 1965, Redenbacher perfected his popcorn hybrid. He had a popcorn that outperformed every other variety in popping volume, pop-ability, and flavor. But his battle wasn't over. It took him another ten years to make his popcorn the best-selling brand in the world. And that's when he and Charlie Bowman sold the brand to Hunt-Wesson Foods.

It would have been easy for Redenbacher to quit his quest for the perfect popcorn. He wasn't successful in marketing it until he was sixty-seven years old. But he had a dream and the determination to pursue it. And he wouldn't give up. When asked about his philosophy, he said, "I've followed the classic homespun principles. Never say die. Never be satisfied. Be stubborn. Be persistent. Integrity is a must. Anything worth having is worth striving for with all your might. Does it sound corny? Honestly, that's all there is to it. There is no magic formula."[2]

If you desire to succeed, realize that there's not much difference between success and failure. If you are willing to be doggedly persistent, you can be a success.

Your Fourteenth Step to Failing Forward:

Understand There's Not Much Difference Between Failure and Success

Take time to write down your dream and the reason why you desire to fulfill it. Then write down all of the things that you would be willing to go through to make it happen. Try to think of everything that could possibly go wrong as you pursue it.

If you do that, you will be mentally prepared for problems to come. And that will help you to be more persistent.

Steps to Failing Forward:

1. Realize there is one major difference between average people and achieving people.

2. Learn a new definition of *failure*.

3. Remove the "you" from failure.

4. Take action and reduce your fear.

5. Change your response to failure by accepting responsibility.

6. Don't let the failure from outside get inside you.

7. Say good-bye to yesterday.

8. Change yourself, and your world changes.

9. Get over yourself and start giving yourself.

10. Find the benefit in every bad experience.

11. If at first you do succeed, try something harder.

12. Learn from a bad experience and make it a good experience.

13. Work on the weakness that weakens you.

14. Understand there's not much difference between failure and success.

15

It's What You Do After You Get Back Up That Counts

Experience is not what happens to you.
Experience is what you do with what happens to you.
—ALDOUS HUXLEY

You are probably familiar with this quote by President Calvin Coolidge. McDonald's founder Ray Kroc used to quote it:

> Nothing in the world can take the place of persistence. Talent will not; nothing is more common than unsuccessful men with talent. Genius will not; unrewarded genius is almost a proverb. Education will not; the world is full of educated derelicts. Persistence and determination alone are omnipotent.

Well, I would have to disagree with that statement. Persistence is important, but it isn't the *only* key to success. I think you need persistence *plus* something more. It's just like the old saying about boxers: A champion gets up one more time than he gets knocked down. Yet if that's the *only* thing he does, he may finally win, but not before getting his brains beaten out. Who wants that? He's much better off if he needs to get up off the canvas only a few times. He does that by figuring out how to knock out his opponent!

HE DIDN'T PLAY GAMES WITH SUCCESS

That's what Milton Bradley did, in a manner of speaking. He figured out what to do so that he wouldn't continue falling down. He started his career at age twenty as a draftsman. That was in 1856. By 1860, he had earned enough money to buy a printing press and go into business for himself as a lithographer.

His first great product idea was for a lithograph of newly elected President Abraham Lincoln. As soon as he offered the print for sale, the orders flooded in. And he would have kept making money except for one problem: His print was of a clean-shaven Lincoln, but the new president had grown a beard. It nearly ruined Bradley.

While he was trying to cope with his first major setback, he decided to try selling something different: a game. When he was a child, his parents had used games as tools to teach him and his siblings. He had a concept for a game he called the Checkered Game of Life, which taught moral values. He designed the game and printed up copies. It was the first parlor game printed in the United States. The game sold well. In fact, as fast as the handmade games could be produced, customers snapped them up. That first year he sold forty thousand copies!

A NEW FOCUS AND PLAN

That first success gave Bradley a new direction in life. He turned his attention to producing games and other materials that stimulated the mind and instructed people while entertaining them. Primarily that meant games. But it wasn't long before he wanted to expand more intentionally into educational resources. A new concept to America had come across the Atlantic Ocean from Germany called kindergarten, and Bradley became very excited by it.

Bradley saw the educational potential of kindergarten for children and the potential market for materials to teach them. He wanted to be the first person in America to print kindergarten materials in English. He wanted to produce building blocks, art supplies, and other items. He intended to make kindergarten materials his primary focus.

But his business associates objected. Because the company was operating in an economic downturn, they believed that focusing such attention in a risky new area might put the company out of business. Bradley was undeterred. He pushed forward with his plan, and ultimately he achieved remarkable success.

"It took all the faith I could muster," said Bradley, "all the belief in the final triumph of kindergarten principles to pull me through those early years of discouragement, when my business associates and other friends and the annual balance sheets of our bookkeeper were all against me."

In time, Bradley became one of kindergarten's chief proponents. He produced numerous materials and even published the influential journal *Kindergarten Review*. He made a difference in the lives of thousands and thousands of children.

A PLAN FOR AFTER YOU GET BACK UP

Maybe you have developed the persistence and resilience to keep getting up when you get knocked down, but you're getting weary of dragging yourself back onto your feet again and again without making any progress. You may be physically and emotionally exhausted. If so, you need to do more than just get back up. What you need is a plan that will help you determine what to do *after* you've gotten back up. Try using these steps based on the word *FORWARD:*

Finalize Your Goal

In the last chapter, I wrote about the importance of having purpose and developing a desire. The next step is to settle on a definite goal you want to reach. The boxer in the ring who gets back up has this goal: knocking out his opponent. Milton Bradley had this goal: to produce educational products for kindergarten students. You need to determine what your goal is. Recognize this:

> The goal shapes the plan.
> The plan shapes the action.

The action achieves the results.
The results bring success.

If you cannot finalize your goal, you won't be able to turn your failures into successes. George Matthew Adams asserts, "In this life, we get only those things for which we hunt, for which we strive, and for which we are willing to sacrifice. It is better to aim for something you want—even though you miss it—than to get something that you didn't aim to get, and which you don't want! If we look long enough for what we want in life we are almost sure to find it, no matter what that objective may be."

Order Your Plans

The saying is old (it was coined by Benjamin Franklin), but it's true: "By failing to prepare you are preparing to fail." There is no guarantee that what you plan will be carried out in the way you envision it, but if you neglect to plan, your chances of success are very slim.

Novelist Victor Hugo believed, "He who every morning plans the transactions of the day and follows out that plan carries a thread that will guide him through the labyrinth of the most busy life . . . But where no plan is laid, where the disposal of time is surrendered merely to the chance of incident, chaos will soon reign." That is undoubtedly why Spanish author Miguel de Cervantes wrote, "The man who is prepared has his battle half fought."

> **By failing to prepare you are preparing to fail.**
> —BENJAMIN FRANKLIN

Risk Failing by Taking Action

Planning alone won't bring success. The other half of the battle is taking action. Conrad Hilton said, "Success seems to be connected with action. Successful people keep moving."

Moving forward on a plan and actually *doing* it always involves risk. And that's good because nothing of value is achieved without risk. You have to put yourself on the line to reach the finish line. Larry Osborne speaks of risk:

> *Highly successful leaders ignore conventional wisdom and take chances. Their stories inevitably include a defining moment or key decision when they took a significant risk and thereby experienced a breakthrough.*
>
> —*LARRY OSBORNE*

"Highly successful leaders ignore conventional wisdom and take chances. Their stories inevitably include a defining moment or key decision when they took a significant risk and thereby experienced a breakthrough."

Welcome Mistakes

By now, you realize that mistakes are not to be avoided but embraced. They are signals that you're moving into new territory, breaking new ground, making progress. As the old English proverb states, "He who makes no mistakes never makes anything." (If you are still having a hard time with this concept, I recommend that you go back and review the previous chapters. The only way you will be able to fail forward is to accept mistakes as a part of your life, learn from them, and improve.)

Advance Based on Your Character

Every time you face mistakes and attempt to move forward in spite of them is a test of character. There always comes a time when *giving up* is easier than *standing up*, when *giving in* looks more attractive than *digging in*. And in those moments, character may be the only thing you have to draw on to keep you going.

Championship-winning NBA coach Pat Riley said, "There comes a moment that defines winning from losing. The true warrior understands and seizes the moment by giving an effort so intensive and so intuitive that it could be called one from the heart." After you've been knocked down, and you've had the will to get back up, the intelligence to plan your come-back, and the courage to take action, know this: You will experience one of those defining moments. And it will define you—as an achiever or a quitter. Prepare for that moment and know that it's coming—and you increase your chances for winning your way through it.

Reevaluate Your Progress Continually

By fighting through the difficult times and overcoming mistakes, you have the opportunity to learn and adjust. William Knudson joked, "Experience is knowing a lot of things you shouldn't do."

People don't like to examine their mistakes, yet that's what it takes to achieve. Katie Paine, president of Delahaye Medialink, says, "Business culture teaches us never to admit our mistakes but to bury them instead—or to blame somebody else. And most personnel and project reviews don't really do much to uncover mistakes. If we wait until we've finished a project to conduct a postmortem, people will forget the mistake, or they'll build up a grudge against a coworker. Either way we lose a learning opportunity."

> *There comes a moment that defines winning from losing. The true warrior understands and seizes the moment by giving an effort so intensive and so intuitive that it could be called one from the heart.*
>
> —PAT RILEY

Develop New Strategies to Succeed

Lester Thurlow points out that "a competitive world has two possibilities for you. You can lose, or, if you want to win, you can change." Once you develop a plan and put it into action, you're not finished. In fact, if you want to succeed, you're never finished. Success is in the journey, the continual process. And no matter how hard you work, you will not create the perfect plan or execute it without error. You will never get to the point that you no longer make mistakes, that you no longer fail. But that's okay.

Personal finance author and lecturer Robert Kiyosaki acknowledges, "In my own life, I've noticed that winning usually follows losing." One of Kiyosaki's favorite stories comes from the teachings of his friend Mike's dad when he was growing up. He said that the man, whom he called "rich dad," loved Texas and Texans. Rich dad used to say,

If you really want to learn the attitude of how to handle risk, losing and failure, go to San Antonio and visit the Alamo. The Alamo is a great story of brave people who chose to fight, knowing there was no hope of success against overwhelming odds. They chose to die instead of surrendering. It's an inspiring story worthy of study; nonetheless, it's still a tragic military defeat. They got their butts kicked. A failure if you will. They lost. So how do Texans handle failure? They still shout, "Remember the Alamo!"

Kiyosaki adds,

Every time he was afraid of making a mistake, or losing money, he told this story . . . Rich dad knew that failure would only make him stronger and smarter . . . It gave him the courage to cross the line when others backed out. [He said,] "That's why I like Texans so much. They took a great failure and turned it into a tourist destination that makes them millions."[1]

Failures are milestones on the success journey. Each time you plan, risk, fail, reevaluate, and adjust, you have another opportunity to begin again, only better than the last time. As sixty-seven-year-old Thomas Edison said as his laboratory burned to the ground, "Thank goodness all our mistakes were burned up. Now we can start again fresh."

A JEWEL OF THE PACIFIC

Starting over usually isn't easy, to say the least, but it sure can bring incredible results. I was reminded of that on a trip I took to Asia in the fall of 1999. For ten days, a team of my leaders and I traveled to India, Hong Kong, Australia, Singapore, and the Philippines to teach leadership.

My favorite stop on that trip was Singapore. It's incredible. It is the most modern country in the world. We took a tour of the city of Singapore, and our guide, Susanna Foo, told us many things about her country. Its gross domestic product in 1998 was $84 billion (measured in U.S. dollars), and it has a per capita gross national product of $22,800, ninth highest in the world.[2] And Singapore accomplishes this in a country of only 238 square miles—that's about one-fifth the size of Rhode Island!

KNOCKED DOWN!

Singapore started out as part of the Sumatran Srivijaya kingdom, but became part of the British Empire in 1826. For more than a century, it remained among Britain's holdings, interrupted only by a time of Japanese occupation during World War II.

After the war, as the British granted independence to more and more members of their former empire, the people of Singapore began to think about their own independence. The British were skeptical. Singapore had no natural resources and no experience in government. The people desired independence, but culturally they still possessed a colonial mind-set. And on top of that, racial prejudice was rampant.

In 1959, Singapore was granted its independence. But the country didn't do well. That's when the people decided that their best hope was to attach themselves to Malaysia, which they did in 1963. But the Malaysians didn't get along well with the people of Singapore, and after two years, Malaysia severed ties with Singapore. The country's leader, Prime Minister Lee Kuan Yew, felt that the country had been cast adrift—with few prospects and little hope. There was only one thing to do: Work themselves out of their horrible situation.

MOVING FORWARD WITH A PLAN

Lee wrestled with the problem until he had a plan. He was a young leader—only forty-two years old—and unlike most of his countrymen, he was educated. He knew that a turnaround was possible, but it would take a generation to do it. His goal was to create First World conditions in a Third World country. And this is how he decided to do it:

1. *Bring in industry.* His first objective was to bring in industries that would employ many low-skilled workers so that the people would have jobs.

2. *Create public housing.* He wanted to improve the people's quality of living and to inspire them. They would move into better housing, but they would pay for it.

3. *Send people to school.* The only way for the country to improve was for the people to improve themselves. He would make education affordable for everyone.

4. *Set up a banking system.* The goal was nothing short of making Singapore the financial center of Asia.

5. *Encourage international travel.* Singapore would become a business and tourist destination with a world-class airport.

Lee's goal was lofty and his plan ambitious. It would take utter determination to achieve what he dreamed, but even then, he would need help in accomplishing it. He turned to the United Nations for assistance. And though the organization was willing to help, things didn't go smoothly at first. Dr. Albert Winsemius, an industrial and economic adviser from the U.N., visited the country and said, "It was bewildering. There were strikes about nothing. There was a riot every other day and everywhere. My first impression was anything but hopeful."

But Lee and the people of Singapore persevered. First, they received hundreds of millions of dollars in loans from the World Bank, and the countries of England and Japan. Next, they brought in experts from around the world to help them, carefully selecting representatives from countries who led their fields:

• Japan and Germany: technical advisers to set up factories

• Sweden and Holland: experts on banking and financing

• Israel: army advisers

• New Zealand and Australia: air force and naval advisers

Then, they brought in twelve hundred companies from the United States and Japan, including General Electric, IBM, Hewlett-Packard, Philips, Sony, Mitsubishi, Caterpillar, Texas Instruments, Mobil Oil, and others.

SINGAPORE'S STORY IS HER STORY

As our guide, Susanna Foo, told us about her country, she fought back the tears. She had been one of the struggling, uneducated people that the country had helped to make a better life. As a teenager in the 1960s, she had dropped out of high school. But as the country got on track, so did she. She went back to night school and improved herself. Today, in her fifties, she understands the incredible distance she and her country have traveled. She has seen the city of Singapore go from a land of swamp and scrub to a flourishing international city. And she has seen the people go from ignorant and helpless to a rugged, disciplined group of achievers.

Singapore continues to change. The people continue to improve, and they focus a lot of their attention on giving something back. "We are involved in helping Bosnia, Zimbabwe, Turkey, Vietnam, East Timor, and Kuwait," says Susanna. "It is our turn to give back. And because we understand how great the need is, we are willing to go wherever the U.N. asks us to go."

I'm not sure when I will get back to Singapore, but as I left, I realized that I would not forget Susanna Foo or her beautiful city. Because of all the countries and cities I've ever been, no place better exemplified what it means to fail forward.

Your Fifteenth Step in Failing Forward:

Get Up, Get Over It, Get Going

Undoubtedly some great task lies ahead of you. Maybe you suspect that accomplishing it is the key to your purpose, but you've been afraid to tackle it. Perhaps you're worried that you will not be able to overcome the failure that could result from attempting it.

Plan to do it. Don't jump into it frivolously. (If you've tried and failed at it once already, then you probably wouldn't be frivolous.) Get back up on your feet, and use the strategy contained in this chapter to move forward:

*F*inalize your goal.
*O*rder your plans.

*R*isk failing by taking action.
*W*elcome mistakes.
*A*dvance based on your character.
*R*eevaluate your progress continually.
*D*evelop new strategies to succeed.

If you're willing to stay determined, work according to a plan, and keep getting up when you get knocked down, you will be able to achieve your goals—and someday your dreams.

Steps to Failing Forward:

1. Realize there is one major difference between average people and achieving people.

2. Learn a new definition of *failure.*

3. Remove the "you" from failure.

4. Take action and reduce your fear.

5. Change your response to failure by accepting responsibility.

6. Don't let the failure from outside get inside you.

7. Say good-bye to yesterday.

8. Change yourself, and your world changes.

9. Get over yourself and start giving yourself.

10. Find the benefit in every bad experience.

11. If at first you do succeed, try something harder.

12. Learn from a bad experience and make it a good experience.

13. Work on the weakness that weakens you.

14. Understand there's not much difference between failure and success.

15. Get up, get over it, get going.

16

Now You're Ready to Fail Forward

Failure is the hallmark of success. It can be the starting point of a new venture, such as when a baby learns to walk; it has to fall down a lot to learn the new skill. Failure is also the mark of a success you've worked for. When a pole-vaulter finally misses in competition, it shows how far he's come. That failure becomes the starting point for his next effort, proving that failure is not final!
—*DAVE ANDERSON*

Well, now you know all the steps it takes to fail forward. Let's review them again quickly:

1. Realize there is one major difference between average people and achieving people.

2. Learn a new definition of *failure*.

3. Remove the "you" from failure.

4. Take action and reduce your fear.

5. Change your response to failure by accepting responsibility.

6. Don't let the failure from outside get inside you.

7. Say good-bye to yesterday.

8. Change yourself, and your world changes.

9. Get over yourself and start giving yourself.

10. Find the benefit in every bad experience.

11. If at first you do succeed, try something harder.

12. Learn from a bad experience and make it a good experience.

13. Work on the weakness that weakens you.

14. Understand there's not much difference between failure and success.

15. Get up, get over it, get going.

I believe wholeheartedly in these steps. But they probably won't mean a thing to you unless you see them in the life of somebody that you consider to be a lot like you.

Let me introduce you to a friend of mine named Dave Anderson. Dave is an entrepreneur I met at a leadership conference that I taught in Kenosha, Wisconsin. I'm going to tell you a little bit about his story. And along the way I'll point out how many of the events in his life correspond to the steps in failing forward that I've outlined in this book.

Let's start with Dave's profile:

FAMOUS DAVE ANDERSON'S PROFILE

Net Value:
  $30 million
Education:
  Master's degree from Harvard University
    (John F. Kennedy School of Government)
Current Position:
  Chairman, Famous Dave's of America
  3,000+ employees
  Annual Sales: $41.6 million
Family Status:
  Married with two children

Career Highlights:
  Founded Famous Dave's of America and took the company public
    (IPO shares opened at $6.25 and closed at $11.25 the first day)
  Cofounded the Rain Forest Café and took it public
  Named Emerging Entrepreneur of the Year by Ernst and Young
    (sponsored by NASDAQ and *USA Today*)
  Past director and executive vice president of organization judged
    "The Fastest Growing Company in America" by *Fortune* magazine
  Participated in two presidential studies: Jimmy Carter's task force to
    study problems of minorities in small business and Ronald Reagan's
    Commission on Indian Reservation Economies
  Helped create more than 18,000 jobs so far in his career through his
    vision, leadership, and ability to see opportunity
  Founder and chairman of the Mino-Giizhig Endowment Fund for
    Disadvantaged Minority Children (initial gift: $1.4 million)
  Executive Mentor, Carlson School of Business MBA Program at the
    University of Minnesota

That's a pretty impressive résumé, and it doesn't even take into account the dozens of local and national culinary and business awards Dave has received—or his accomplishments as a silversmith and antique collector. Everything Dave has ever touched has turned to gold, right? Wrong! To really understand and appreciate Dave's achievements, you need to know more about his failures.

A TYPICAL TEENAGER

When Dave Anderson graduated from high school in 1971, he was like many other eighteen-year-old kids. He wasn't sure what he wanted to do with his life. And if you had suggested to him back then that he would someday be a successful businessman worth tens of millions of dollars making a positive impact on the lives of thousands of people, he probably would have thought you were crazy. Yet that's what has happened to him, and it's all because he's a man who learned how to *fail forward.*

Dave grew up in the city of Chicago. He was an average student, and when he got out of school, he was looking for direction. He wasn't much of a people person, so he was thinking in terms of finding a career where he could be outdoors and be closer to nature. Because of his Native American heritage (his father is Choctaw and his mother is Chippewa), he considered a career in wildlife and forestry. He went to Michigan Tech University in Houghton, Michigan, and started living the typical college experience—some class work and studying during the week with lots of partying on the weekends.

Opportunity Came Calling

During the break after his first term, he went back to Chicago to visit his parents, and a friend called him.

"Dave," he asked. "You got a suit?"

"Yeah, you know I do," Dave responded. He'd grown up going to church, and in those days that's what you wore.

"Well, put it on and I'll pick you up," his friend said.

Back then Dave was ready for anything, so he put on his suit, and when his buddy picked him up, they went to a meeting recruiting people to sell an oil conditioner for automobile engines. Dave wasn't a mechanically inclined guy, so the technical part of the presentation didn't connect with him. But he was really excited by the speaker, a fellow named Zig Ziglar, who told him and the other men and women in attendance, "If you believe in yourself and have passion, you can succeed."

Dave had never really heard anything like that before in school or at home. His parents loved him, but they didn't know much about positive motivation and they weren't entrepreneurs. His dad was a construction worker who worked hard at his job and encouraged his son to do the same.

That night Dave went home and talked to his parents about the opportunity of selling that product, and when the company held its next meeting, Dave went back and took his dad along. It seemed like a viable opportunity to him, and he certainly wanted to see his son succeed. So he put $2,500 of his hard-earned money into buying the product for Dave to start him in business.

DAVE'S FIRST BUSINESS

Dave never went back to Michigan Tech. For the first time in his life, he had a dream, and he had bought into it 100 percent. He wanted to be a success and make it in business. For the next few months, he worked as hard as he could to sell that oil conditioner. But it was as if he'd hit a brick wall. No matter how hard he tried, he couldn't make it work. It was his first business failure. Dave says that as far as he knows, his dad still has a few cases of that oil conditioner stockpiled somewhere in his garage.

But contained within that first big failure were seeds of his future success. (Step 15: Get up, get over it, get going.) First, he had hope. He believed that he *could* be successful. (Step 6: Don't let the failure from outside get inside you.) Second, when his dad bought the product for him, Dave received a five-day leadership course that he says changed his life. (Step 10: Find the benefit in every bad experience.) He also was given six tapes by Zig Ziglar. Every night for months, Dave went to sleep listening to those tapes. (Step 8: Change yourself, and your world changes.) The dream within him wasn't dead. And he wasn't going to let that failure get him down. (Step 1: Realize there is one major difference between average people and achieving people.) He just wouldn't realize success through that business.

After failing as an oil conditioner entrepreneur, Dave went to work part-time selling sporting goods for Eddie Bauer. And in the fall of 1972, he enrolled in Roosevelt University in Chicago. For the next several years, like clockwork, Dave enrolled at Roosevelt in the fall and ended up with a bunch of zeros and incompletes on his transcript. He had the desire to improve himself, but a weak aptitude for school, coupled with the demands of various business ventures, caused him to fail in his desire to get an education.

ANOTHER VENTURE

It was also in 1972 that Dave got the idea for another business. Although the oil additive opportunity didn't work for him, it encouraged him to start thinking like an entrepreneur. (Step 2: Learn a new definition of *failure*.) His idea was to create and sell miniature dish gardens. He scraped together a few dollars and bought the materials to make up a few samples. Then he went out and talked to retailers, trying to get them to buy them.

Dave had his first bit of success with James Ashner at Richard Lange Florist. He told Dave, "These look good. Okay, let me have a dozen of this one, a dozen of these, and a dozen of these," pointing to his favorites.

Dave was stunned. "That's a lot of money," he said, quickly calculating the cost of materials in his head. "How about one of each?"

"No," said Ashner, "I want a dozen of these, a dozen of these, and a dozen of this one too."

"You sure you don't just want to take one of each?" Dave offered timidly. He figured that if he could sell and deliver a few of his samples, he would have enough money to buy supplies.

"No," Ashner replied simply.

"I can't get you a dozen of each," Dave finally explained. "I don't have enough money to buy the materials to make them."

"Well, you look like an honest guy. What if I pay you up front? Would that help?" Ashner answered. "Ann Marie," he called to his assistant in the next room, "write this guy a check."

Dave was dumbfounded. A few minutes later, in his hands was the largest check he'd ever held. It was for $736.35.

ANOTHER GAIN

That was the day Dave started his wholesale florist business. For the next seven years, he operated out of his basement and worked like a madman. He put in long hours seven days a week. When his retail florist customers experienced their heavy crunch times around Mother's Day and Valentine's Day, he went into their shops, swept up, cleaned out coolers, and did other chores to help them out. By age twenty-one, he had accounts with every major retail florist in the city of Chicago. By his late twenties, he felt like a tremendous success.

Around that time a florist friend had an idea to make some extra money. Back in the late seventies, students at universities liked to decorate their dorm rooms and apartments with plants. Dave's friend, whose son attended Southern Illinois University, figured that they could buy plants cheap from the grower in Florida, rent space in the student union at the beginning of the fall term, and sell the plants at a hefty profit. And that's what they did. They drove to Florida with a semi, filled it up with plants, and brought them back. They were able to eliminate two middlemen from the process, mark the plants up in price, and still sell them for much less than the usual retail price. They made $20,000 in two days! (Step 11: If at first you do succeed, try something harder.)

AND ANOTHER LOSS

Because that venture had brought such success, they were ready to try it again, but this time on a larger scale. A new Kmart was scheduled to open in Pontiac, Illinois, in October, and they made arrangements to sell plants there. Dave and his friend went to Florida and brought back two semis full of plants. They rented a big tent, filled it up with plants, and set up four cash registers to wait on customers. But a funny thing happened that day. A strange fog drifted in. Then it started to drizzle. Before long, the drizzle turned into a steady rain. That's when it suddenly turned cold. The rain became sleet and then snow. Winter had come early, and the tender tropical plants couldn't take it. They lost everything. The venture cost them the $20,000 they had made in the prior student sale plus other money they had put into it.

If you're from the Midwest, you probably remember the winter of 1979. It was one of the worst on record. The snowstorm that hit Chicago was horrible, and the drifts were so high that many side streets were closed *for months*. A lot of businesses went under that year—including Dave's. Florists don't buy much in the middle of a blizzard. Many of Dave's customers not only weren't buying from him, they also weren't paying him the money they owed for orders they had already received. That, coupled with the huge loss at Kmart, put him under. He filed for bankruptcy.

IN SEARCH OF NEW STRENGTHS

After Dave lost his business, he needed to find a job to support himself. More than once he had to pawn his wife's jewelry to pay the rent. Twice he stood in line to file for unemployment, but he walked out, determined never to accept a check from the government. He kept looking. Because he had always worked for himself, he wanted to find something that would allow him to use his entrepreneurial spirit. But he also wanted something that would help him improve himself. All successful people, he reasoned, had good people skills, and he felt that his ability to work with people still needed to be strengthened. (Step 13: Work on the weakness that weakens you.) Those two desires meant one thing: He needed to take a sales job—and that scared him. His fear of failure in that area was overwhelming.

He landed a job working for the American Can Company, selling Dixie cups, Marathon paper towels, and tissue to restaurants. (Step 4: Take action and reduce your fear.) To get his foot in the door, he took the worst territory. At night, when his family was out of the house, he would practice talking, smiling, and even shaking hands with himself in front of a mirror. During the day, he worked hard. He relied on the same principles and tenacity he had in the wholesale floral industry. (Step 14: Understand there's not much difference between failure and success.) He made a lot of mistakes, experienced much rejection, and lost many sales. But he worked like crazy and kept learning. In six months, he took a territory that had been in last place and made it number one in the company.

He learned a lot in that position. He discovered that "you have to experience a lot of failure to achieve success. And the more failure you go through, the higher your success." He also discovered that his past failure didn't brand him for life. (Step 3: Remove the "you" from failure.)

"After I lost my [wholesale floral] business, I went back to some of the companies I had worked with before," says Dave. "All I could think about was the thousands of dollars I owed them when I filed for bankruptcy. But they didn't care about that. Their thought was, 'We wrote that off years ago. Besides, we made a lot more than that from you during our years doing business together.' [Step 7: Say good-bye to yesterday.] You know, if you're honest and admit your failures, people are pretty forgiving. People want to help you if you take responsibility for yourself." (Step 5: Change your response to failure by accepting responsibility.)

OPPORTUNITY AGAIN?

In 1982, Dave's tribe, the Lac Courte Orielles Lake Superior Band of Ojibwa in northwest Wisconsin, came calling. Their organization was losing money, and recognizing his business prowess, they asked him to be their CEO. That put him in charge of a variety of businesses and interests, including a cranberry marsh, a print shop, and a construction company. He led the tribe's concerns for three years. During that time, gross revenues increased from $3.9 million to more than $8 million.

His success with his tribe prompted President Reagan to recognize Dave in the Commission on Indian Reservation Economies. Various state and local government and business organizations honored him and asked him to sit on numerous councils for areas such as tourism and minority business development. In time, Dave was helping so many people that he was granted a Bush Leadership Fellowship for a lifetime of outstanding achievement by the Bush Foundation in St. Paul, Minnesota. That's how he got into Harvard—with no undergraduate degree and a transcript full of poor grades.

After he graduated, he worked with the Mille Lacs Tribe for several years. Dave helped them create thousands of jobs, bringing their previously devastating unemployment rate down to nearly zero, and helped build the company that *Fortune* magazine recognized as the fastest growing in America. Though Dave had achieved success in a variety of businesses, he had not yet done anything related to his true passion: food.

PURSUING HIS LOVE

Dave's love for food began when he was just a kid. His father worked at various construction sites around Chicago as an electrician, and he occasionally brought home leftover ribs from one of the storefront barbecue shacks introduced to him by a coworker. As soon as Dave tasted his first rib, he was hooked. And as soon as he was old enough to work, he started what he calls "the quest for the perfect barbecue." Every place he traveled to around the country for business, he talked to the locals to find out where the best restaurants were.

"I've traveled the back roads and side streets of this country searching for great-tasting food," says Dave enthusiastically. "I've been everywhere from storefront kitchens down inner-city side streets to country road houses to fine dining restaurants. When I'd go to a convention, after fulfilling my company obligations, I'd disappear, and my coworkers would wonder where I was. I was in the best little restaurants in town. I'd order everything on the menu and taste it all. Then I'd go home and experiment in my own kitchen."

In 1994, Dave cofounded a highly successful restaurant company called the Rain Forest Café, and it made him wealthy. He used some of the money he made to purchase a small resort in Hayward, Wisconsin. There Dave built the kind of restaurant he'd always dreamed of having: one that made great barbecue. He was going to call it Dave's Famous Barbecue, but the printer made a mistake and printed FAMOUS DAVE'S and the name stuck. The restaurant was a huge success. Soon he opened a second Famous Dave's, then another.

At this point, if you didn't know better, you'd think Dave was set. But he was on the verge of facing the lowest point of his life and his greatest obstacle—himself.

HE GOT THE TREATMENT

In 1995, a group of friends and family came to Dave in what's commonly called an intervention. In other words, they confronted him about his drinking. Dave had started drinking in college, as many people do. But he didn't leave it behind when he moved into the business world. When the people who loved him called him on the carpet, he was secretly pleased because he knew he needed to change. He went into treatment for alcoholism, and he's been sober ever since.

"The key to making it through treatment and succeeding is accepting that you have a problem—that you drink too much—accepting where you are, and moving on from there," Dave asserts. "The people who go through treatment and don't stay sober fail because they believe they're right. They won't take responsibility for themselves. The key to change is surrender."

Dave knew he needed to change, and in the years since he turned his life around, he has seen lots of change in himself. Now continual learning and growth are the hallmarks of his life. (Step 12: Learn from a bad experience and make it a good experience.)

"I realized that I couldn't hang around with my drinking friends and change," he says. "If I went back to the bar where I used to drink, I know the same people would still be there sitting in the same places. They wouldn't have changed a bit. But I've changed a *lot* in four years."

IT'S NOT ABOUT DAVE

As I write this, Dave owns twenty-four restaurants in five states. And the business is still growing. But to succeed, he has had to overcome a lot of obstacles—and a lot of doubters.

Famous Dave's Corporate Growth

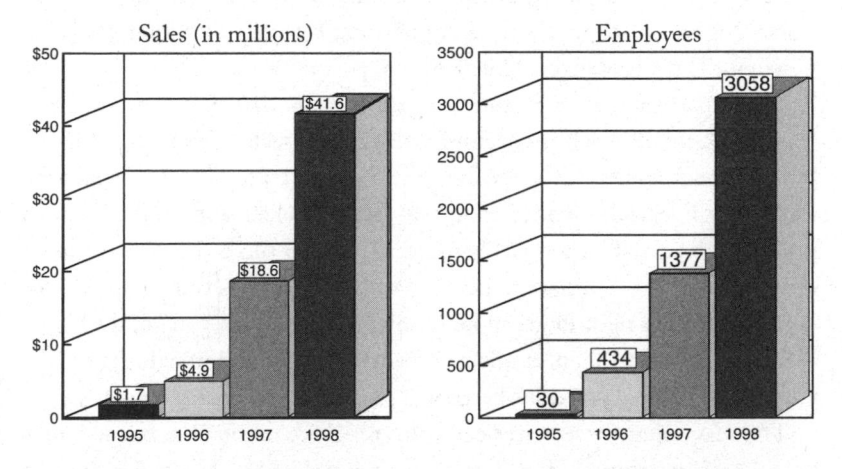

"When I got started, people told me that my restaurants would never go in this part of the country," says Dave. "They said, 'Minneapolis is not a barbecue town. It'll never work.' Well, today I've got thirteen restaurants in Minneapolis."

As incredible as Dave's achievement has been, what's even more remarkable is his realization that his success exists not for himself alone, but for others. He's doing that through the Mino-Giizhig Endowment Fund for Disadvantaged Minority Children, which he founded, and also through Famous Dave's. He confirms, "Our business is more about changing lives than selling ribs." (Step 9: Get over yourself and start giving yourself.)

To help him accomplish that, Dave developed Hog Heaven University where he trains his people. There new managers learn skills, techniques, and information that will help them succeed at Famous Dave's, such as what Dave calls the trinity of barbecue: meat, smoke, and sauce. But they learn something else that's much more important. Dave tells all of them, "This is not about Dave Anderson. This is *your* opportunity."

> *To succeed, you have to be open to problems. You have to be open to failure. And as you go up the ladder, you gain the right to get more problems.*
>
> —DAVE ANDERSON

A key part of that opportunity is knowing how to fail forward. Dave explains, "Schools teach the technical disciplines such as math and science, but not about mental health. What they need to teach is how to deal with problems. Every day you're going to get whacked and thumped with problems. Some of us get jackhammered. But to succeed, you have to be open to problems. You have to be open to failure. And as you go up the ladder, you gain the right to get more problems. The higher you go, the bigger the problems. But the most effective people have gone through the toughest times. They say you don't become a great sailor by sailing calm seas."

The seas definitely haven't been calm for Dave in the past, nor will they be calm in the future. But that doesn't bother him. Obstacles are just opportunities. Dave emphasizes, "I tell my employees all the time: 'Most people run from problems. If you want to get ahead, go to your manager, and say, "You got problems? Give me some." Instead of running from problems like most people, go after them. If you do, I'll guarantee, it will change your life!' That's the way you get ahead, by solving problems."

NOW YOU'RE READY

Dave Anderson has made more mistakes, suffered more adversity, overcome more problems, and experienced more failures than most people you'll ever meet. But he has also achieved more. And as my friend Zig Ziglar declares, "Dave Anderson is just getting started."

The next time you find yourself envying what successful people have achieved, recognize that they have probably gone through many negative experiences that you cannot see on the surface. An old joke goes like this: "Never ask what's in a hot dog while you're eating one." The idea is that if you did know what's in it, you'd never want to eat one again. A lot of failure goes into success.

If you really want to achieve your dreams—I mean *really* achieve them, not just daydream or talk about them—you've got to get out there and fail. Fail early, fail often, but always fail forward. Turn your mistakes into stepping-stones for success.

As I was finishing this book, I sent Dave the first draft of his story so that he could make sure that I'd gotten the details right. A few days later, he sent a note. It said, "I've never seen my life story so laid out before. It's a wonder I never gave up."

Now that you know how to fail forward, you won't have to give up either. I wish you well. Keep dreaming, and keep failing forward.

Notes

Chapter 1

1. Andy Andrews, ed., "Mary Kay Ash," in *Storms of Perfection 2* (Nashville: Lightning Crown Publishers, 1994), 161.

2. "Mary Kay, Inc.," *The Industry Standard* <www.thestandard.net>, August 12, 1999.

Chapter 2

1. Robert M. McMath and Thom Forbes, *What Were They Thinking?* (New York: Random House, 1998).

2. Patricia Sellers, "Now Bounce Back!" *Fortune,* May 1, 1995, 50–51.

3. Philippians 4:11 NKJV.

Chapter 3

1. Andy Andrews, ed., "Erma Bombeck" in *Storms of Perfection 2* (Nashville: Lightning Crown Publishers, 1994), 51.

2. Brad Bushman and Roy Baumeister, *20/20,* August 8, 1999, <www.abcnews.com>.

3. Brodin, "The Key to Bouncing Back," *Discipleship Journal,* issue 109, 1999, 67.

4. "Where Failures Get Fixed," *Fortune,* May 1, 1995, 64.

5. Rudy Ruettiger and Mike Celizic, *Rudy's Rules* (Waco, TX: WRS Publishing, 1995).

Chapter 4

1. Emerson Klees, *Entrepreneurs in History—Success vs. Failure: Entrepreneurial Role Models* (Rochester, NY: Cameo Press, 1995), 202.

2. Ibid., 203.

3. Patrick Kavanaugh, *The Spiritual Lives of the Great Composers* (Nashville: Sparrow Press, 1992), 5.

Chapter 5

1. Gary Hamel and C. K. Prahalad, *Competing for the Future* (Boston: Harvard Business School Press, 1994), 51–52.

2. Jeff Schultz, "The Price of Success," *Atlanta Journal-Constitution*, January 6, 1999, E4.

3. David Goldman, "Shocking, Lurid, and True!" *Biography*, April 1998, 14.

Chapter 6

1. Interview with Greg Horn, P.O. Box 175, Hwy. 27 South, Cynthiana, Kentucky 41031.

2. *Fortune*, May 1, 1995, 50.

3. Lucinda Hahn, "What Makes Them So Tough?" *Reader's Digest*, November 1998, 88–93.

4. Roger Crawford and Michael Bowker, *Playing from the Heart: A Portrait in Courage* (Rocklin, CA: Prima Publishing, 1997), 28–32.

5. Roger Crawford, *How High Can You Bounce? Turn Setbacks into Comebacks* (New York: Bantam Books, 1998), 8.

6. Crawford and Bowker, *Playing from the Heart*, 12.

Chapter 7

1. Bert Randolf Sugar, *The 100 Greatest Athletes of All Time* (Secaucus, NJ: Citadel Press, 1995), 217.

2. Allan Zullo with Chris Rodell, *When Bad Things Happen to Good Golfers: Pro Golf's Greatest Disasters* (Kansas City: Andrews McMeel, 1998), 40–43.

3. Dick Biggs, *Burn Brightly Without Burning Out* (Successories Library, 1998), 30–31.

Chapter 8

1. Garry Marshall with Lori Marshall, "Stand Out from the Crowd," *Reader's Digest*, 61.

Chapter 9

1. Lloyd Cory, *Quotable Quotations* (Wheaton, IL: Victor Books, 1985), 347.

2. Rebecca Lamar Harmon, *Susanna: Mother of the Wesleys* (Nashville: Abingdon Press, 1968), 57.

Chapter 10

1. David Bayles and Ted Orland, *Art and Fear: Observations on the Perils (And Rewards) of Artmaking* (Santa Barbara: Capra Press, 1993), 29.

2. Arthur Freeman and Rose Dewolf, *Woulda, Coulda, Shoulda: Overcoming Regrets, Mistakes, and Missed Opportunities* (New York: Harper Collins, 1992).

3. Patricia Sellers, "Now Bounce Back!" *Fortune*, May 1, 1995, 49.

4. Lloyd Ogilvie, *Falling into Greatness* (Nashville: Thomas Nelson, 1984).

5. Genesis 40:14–15 NIV.

Chapter 11

1. "Amelia Earhart: 1897–1937," <www.noahsays.com>.

2. "Amelia Earhart," <www.ionet.net>.

3. "Quotes," <www.cmgww.com>.

4. "Amelia Earhart," <www.ionet.net>.

5. "Quotes," <www.cmgww.com>.

6. *The Joyful Noiseletter.*

7. Gloria Lau, "Joseph Lister, Developer of Antiseptic Surgery," *Investor's Business Daily,* January 22, 1999, A5.

8. Norman B. Medow, "Ounce of Prevention a Lesson Worth Learning," *Ophthalmology Times,* April 15, 1997, 12.

Chapter 12

1. "Surviving Everest Heightens Texan's Priorities About Life," *Atlanta Journal-Constitution,* November 14, 1998, E22.

2. Michael E. Young, "The Ultimate Challenge: Climber Left for Dead on Everest Learns to Cherish Life As Never Before," *Dallas Morning News,* May 11, 1997.

3. "Surviving Everest Heightens Texan's Priorities About Life."

4. Jim Zabloski, *The 25 Most Common Problems in Business* (Nashville: Broadman and Holman, 1996), 88.

Chapter 13

1. "Luck Rivals Worst of Sick Jokes: 'There's Hope,' New Yorker Says," *Los Angeles Times,* March 19, 1995, A28. Copyright Reuters Limited 1995.

2. Carole Hyatt and Linda Gottlieb, *When Smart People Fail* (New York: Penguin Books, 1993).

3. David Bayles and Ted Orland, *Art and Fear: Observations on the Perils (And Rewards) of Artmaking* (Santa Barbara: Capra Press, 1993), 27–28.

Chapter 14

1. "Quitters, Campers and Climbers," *Sky,* October 1998, 103.

2. Len Sherman, *Popcorn King: How Orville Redenbacher and His Popcorn Charmed America* (Arlington: Summit Publishing Group, 1996).

Chapter 15

1. Robert T. Kiyosaki with Sharon L. Lechter, *Rich Dad, Poor Dad* (Paradise Valley, AZ: Cashflow Education Australia, 1997), 135–36.

2. "About the Singapore Economy," <www.gov.fg>.

About the Author

John C. Maxwell is an internationally recognized leadership expert, speaker, and author who has sold over 12 million books. His organizations have trained more than one million leaders worldwide. Dr. Maxwell is the founder of Injoy Stewardship Services and EQUIP. Every year he speaks to Fortune 500 companies, international government leaders, and organizations as diverse as the United States Military Academy at West Point and the National Football League. A *New York Times*, *Wall Street Journal*, and *Business Week* best-selling author, Maxwell was one of 25 authors named to Amazon.com's 10th Anniversary Hall of Fame. Two of his books, *The 21 Irrefutable Laws of Leadership* and *Developing the Leader Within You*, have each sold over a million copies.

Books by Dr. John C. Maxwell
Can Teach You How to Be A **REAL** Success

RELATIONSHIPS

Be a People Person

Becoming a Person of Influence

Relationships 101

The Power of Influence

The Power of Partnership in the Church

The Treasure of a Friend

Ethics 101

Winning with People

25 Ways to Win with People

EQUIPPING

Developing the Leaders Around You

Equipping 101

The 17 Indisputable Laws of Teamwork

The 17 Essential Qualities of a Team Player

Partners in Prayer

Your Road Map for Success

Success One Day at a Time

Today Matters

Talent Is Never Enough

ATTITUDE

Be All You Can Be

Failing Forward

The Power of Thinking Big

Living at the Next Level

Think on These Things

The Winning Attitude

Your Bridge to a Better Future

The Power of Attitude

Attitude 101

Thinking for a Change

The Difference Maker

The Journey from Success to Significance

LEADERSHIP

The 21 Indispensable Qualities of a Leader

The 21 Irrefutable Laws of Leadership

The 21 Most Powerful Minutes in a Leader's Day

Developing the Leader Within You

Leadership 101

Leadership Promises for Every Day

The 360 Degree Leader

The Right to Lead